A BOY REMEMBERS

This book is dedicated to all those men and women who fought to bring peace to the world and liberation to the Channel Islands.

"OLD MEN FORGET, YET ALL SHALL BE FORGOT
BUT HE'LL REMEMBER WITH ADVANTAGES
WHAT FEATS HE DID THAT DAY"
Henry V before Agincourt.
William Shakespeare

Author   Leo Harris

The moral rights of the author has been asserted
All rights reserved, unauthorised duplication
contravenes applicable laws

First Published   November 2000
Reprinted   January 2001

Publisher   Apache Guides Limited
                   Apache House
                   Route de St. Aubin
                   St. Helier
                   Jersey. JE2 3SG

Printed by   Deltor Ltd
                   Long Acre
                   Saltash
                   Cornwall PL12 6LZ

Production   Deltor Ltd

Copyright   A Boy Remembers
I S B N   903469-02-3
A catalogue record of this book is available from the British Library

D1422295

Holder (Inhaber) **HARRIS**
Andrew Leo
Residing at (Wohnhaft) Hotel Marina,
Havredesttes St Helier.
Born on the (Geboren am) 14/10/1930 at Edinburgh, (in) Scotland.

Leo in September 1944

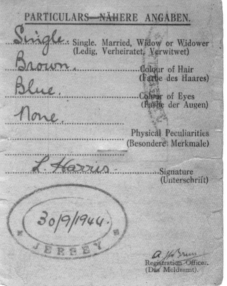

PARTICULARS—NÄHERE ANGABEN.

Single. : Single. Married, Widow or Widower (Ledig, Verheiratet, Verwitwet)

Brown. Colour of Hair (Farbe des Haares)

Blue. Colour of Eyes (Farbe der Augen)

None Physical Peculiarities (Besondere Merkmale)

L Harris Signature (Unterschrift)

30/9/1944.

JERSEY

A. Le Brun
Registration Officer.
(Das Meldeamt).

CONTENTS

My Father John F. Harris in the 1930's

My Brother Francis in 1951

PREFACE

I have not attempted to write a History of the Occupation of Jersey in the pages which follow, I am only recording my own personal experiences as a boy living in the Island in those troubled times. There are no notes or diaries to work from as I never kept any, but my memory is crystal clear about the events as I saw them.

My father was an unusual man and very little that he did could be construed as following the others. He was fiercely independent and a good deal of this rubbed off onto my older brother, Francis. So, in many ways this is their story told through the eyes of a small boy watching closely from the background. To them and to my mother, who supported us with tremendous courage, I partly dedicate this work.

Both Francis and I are agreed that the greatest tribute is due to the people of Jersey who supported our family with their concern, friendship and material goods with great generosity. We were newcomers to the Island, caught up in the avalanche of war as the German army swept over Europe in 1940 and yet we were accepted as friends by so many of the Islanders. There are too many to mention here by name, but our thanks goes out to all of them and to prove our appreciation we returned to the Island in 1946 to settle permanently.

The British Broadcasting Corporation must also receive their due measure of thanks for the inspired broadcasting to occupied Europe, which took place throughout the war. Those responsible can never know how much it meant to all of us to hear the truth, and warm English voices above the harsh and guttural commands of our oppressors. I record here our profound thanks to all of them.

Finally and most importantly, we wish to give our thanks to the many brave men and women who fought so that our Liberation would take place one day.

Francis in June 1944

Mother and Father

The Brothers at Elizabeth Castle before the war

The Marina Hotel about 1937

An Introduction

It is not easy to write about my father, not that I did not like him, for as a boy I loved him very much; it is because I fear that you, the reader, will find it tedious and ordinary. And yet I must write about him for he is central to my account of the German Occupation of Jersey as I saw it as a boy. My father was strange, if you judge him by other men. He was a very private person and could be oversensitive to criticism and yet he used his native wit and instinctive engineering skill to build a fine business in the Edinburgh of 1919.

Born in Ayrshire, into the Winn-Harris family which had fled Kent when they had turned Catholic at a time when to deny the established Church of England carried severe penalties and restrictions. He grew up in a family which had changed from serving its country in the Navy and become Ayrshire farmers, made welcome in Scotland. John Francis Winn-Harris was born in Ayr on September 14, 1892 into a large family, one of the youngest among several brothers and sisters. His father signed the birth certificate as Theatrical Manager, but this must have been among his other attributes as he certainly farmed and he gave his address as 'The Old Mansion House'.

The internal combustion engine and steam traction engines breathed life into my father's spirit. He was sensitive to the slightest whim or hint of trouble from his beloved machinery. I have seen him stop beside a car in 1930's Edinburgh as the owner parked it in Prince's Street and advise the driver that a sparkplug lead was off or loose, he could hear it 'ticking' as the engine was running.

A volunteer into the Royal Engineers in 1914, his army career remains something of a mystery. He never discussed it after the war and it was only by chance that a letter he wrote from a Scottish Mission hut 'behind the lines' while his company were resting, came to light after his death in 1974. He used to pass off his army days as having spent them at Woolwich Arsenal, but he had certainly met Marie Lloyd and driven her car around London. It was also known that he used large traction engines to deliver guns which had been used in France, to be War Memorials in towns in England and later, in 1919, had removed explosives from coal mines and quarries, some of it in dangerous condition, during the General Strike.

So it was that he came back to Edinburgh in 1919 and by 1920 had started up in business with a 'motorworks' in Leith and eventually a coach service named 'The White Line'. 'The Morning Post', one of Edinburgh's leading newspapers, has recently published letters about John Winn-Harris's exploits in Court against the Edinburgh Corporation, when that worthy body unfairly tried to restrain his enterprising spirit.

He married Anne Catherine Maria Josephine Kilcoyne in London in 1925 and Francis, my brother, was born in 1927. I followed in 1930 and began to grow up in a warm, close family surrounded by beautiful cars. I often feel for Mr Toad in the 'Wind in the Willows', how I understand his passion for the car, this supreme engineering achievement which gave mankind its first taste of true mobility.

The business prospered, the coaches were sold and a new, very fine garage business was built on the main road North out of Edinburgh, with fourteen electric petrol pumps on a large forecourt, which sat between two roads, one into Edinburgh, the other into the port of Leith. In 1936, my father accepted a good price for his business and, searching round for a new 'exploit', settled on Jersey and a certain aquarium at Havre-des-Pas.

The Marina Hotel was soon opened and the main room of the aquarium became the restaurant with its front entrance straight off the promenade. The family remained in Edinburgh while all this took place and Francis and I used to look forward eagerly to my father's return after a prolonged absence. At last the day came when we all arrived in Jersey to see the hotel and we spent a wonderful holiday staying in a little chalet in the grounds of the house next door, ' Rocquaine'.

We returned in 1938 and again in 1939 aboard a sombre, camouflaged Mailboat as the ferries were then called. I believe it was the Isle of Sark. I know we zigzagged all night to avoid submarines. This was an odd visit. Francis and I were to go back to school in Edinburgh in 1940 and all due preparations were made. Would you believe it, we were booked on the mailboat with our car, a Rover, as people were queuing to be evacuated aboard colliers.

However, this was not to be. We were living in a rented terraced house at the bottom of St. Saviours Hill, when on a fine summer, day a man came to see my father to tell him that the hotel manager, a Mr. Marett and his family had all evacuated leaving the building wide open. My father hurried off to effect the closure of the hotel. Our car sailed without us. Six months later when we had not arrived in Southampton, the Rover and all our luggage was sold by the Automobile Association for £6, this in the middle of the Blitz as the Luftwaffe tried to hit the docks and Supermarine Aircraft Factory.

The first stage of our Occupation has begun. I was nearly ten years old.

My Father's business in Edinburgh (1933) fourteen shops and a garage

4

The Marina Café - Looking towards the promenade (1937)

The Marina Hotel in 1945

The Occupation begins

Chapter One　　　　THE OCCUPATION BEGINS

It was decided that the family would move into the Marina Hotel. I was excited, at the thought of living in a large building with thirty bedrooms, a huge kitchen and a restaurant, it seemed to a boy of nearly ten, to be quite an adventure and so it turned out to be. Francis and I were able to swim directly from the hotel with the sea at high tide lapping the promenade. We found an outdoor kiosk attached to the restaurant with a large counter bordering the promenade. Everything was there and in working order. We made milkshakes and Horlicks on electrical equipment and dispensed free service to our few customers in this phoney war.

The sun shone down and nothing happened to disturb our days. Then, one Sunday morning, we had just returned from church when we became aware of a black cloud that grew on the horizon towards St. Malo. The cloud stayed on the horizon, but steadily increased in size. It looked like an approaching storm, but we had never seen a cloud like this. Could anything have been more ominous? We knew that the German army was very close and all the stories which had filled, not only the newspapers, but also our boys' comics, were heavily laden with lurid descriptions of German atrocities.

We later discovered that the black cloud was indeed a portent of what was to come, as it was caused by the burning of the oil storage tanks in St. Malo by our own retreating troops. I also learned many years later of the brave little fleet of Jersey yachts, which sailed at twenty-four hours notice to St. Malo to take off the demolition parties from under the very noses of the German troops then entering the outskirts of St. Malo.

One glorious day, while my father was busy putting in place the shutters that normally protected the glazed entrance of the restaurant from the sea, Francis and I amused ourselves on the promenade, which still held an attraction for a few people enjoying the view and a stroll. The drone of distant aircraft, not an uncommon sound in those days, came up from the east and looking up we saw three aircraft in Vee formation glinting in the sun. They were a little way offshore over the sea and only attracted our attention as, like many boys, we liked to identify types of aircraft. As they steadily approached a whistling noise, quite faint, but clearly associated with the planes, became increasingly apparent and streaks, like contrails, appeared beneath them.

"Quick, get inside," it was my father's voice, " they're bombing us." He had moved towards us as the planes had approached, interested to share in our discussion. Now his earlier experience of war had awakened at the sound. We scampered into the building while he ran along the promenade calling out to everyone he could see to get into our restaurant for cover. Having been an aquarium before its conversion, the walls of the restaurant were thick and a series of broad, fan-shaped steps led down off the promenade into a cheerful interior. The tables around the sides nestled in alcoves, which at one time were the glass-fronted tanks, which held the marine life. "Under the tables everyone," and we all got under the sturdy tables with their black, square legs. I can still see the view between the legs, through the open doors, across the promenade and past the stout iron railings to the beach.

We waited. It only took a minute or two and suddenly the ground shook and everything rattled. Then there was a very loud bang followed by a succession of shakes and bangs. Aircraft engines roared in the distance and we could hear machinegun fire. At last it stopped and, after a while, my father went outside to see if the sky was clear. We emerged, quite shaken, from our table shelters and looked outside.

Our guests quickly said their thanks and went hurrying homeward. Beyond the hotel, about a quarter of a mile to the north, a column of smoke rose alongside Fort Regent, but otherwise there was nothing to be seen in our vicinity

Later, we walked along sunny roads with my father and, climbing Mount Bingham, saw a large bomb crater near the Ropewalk. The soil thrown up by the explosion was quite warm to the touch and I pulled out a large piece of shrapnel from the bomb weighing about two pounds. A man had been washing his car outside his house nearby, we were told by onlookers and had been killed. We walked on down to the harbour and could see the marks of bullets in the granite of the pavement and on the walls. Again we were told that a man sheltering in the alcoves in the wall opposite the La Folie had been shot. It was also rumoured that a ship in the harbour had fired at the attacking aircraft with its stern mounted anti-aircraft gun.

The smouldering keels of several small fishing boats lay on the dry harbour bed in the Old harbour, their engines and metal gear standing out starkly above the smoking planks and ribs. Several yachts were badly damaged too. They all lay there for the rest of the war.

A strange silence now settled over the island. Havre-des-Pas became a quiet place as our fate approached. Then it was on us, the Germans were about to land and all buildings were to fly white flags or face German fire. The streets were soon full of sheets and pillowcases hanging out on makeshift 'flagpoles'. This gave us a terrible sense of shame and inferiority and was, as we later discovered, a mistake caused by the misinterpretation of the German surrender instructions to the civil authority which had been dropped on the airport by a low flying Luftwaffe plane.

Schools were closed. Shops were selling out of stocks of food and clothing. Francis and I visited the pier to look at the empty berths from which the evacuees had left; the empty and abandoned cars and carts silent witnesses of their flight. It was eerie, yet exciting, like moving through the stages of a continuing nightmare.

My father had been asked to close up some of the houses, which lay open to the winds after the precipitate flight of their occupants. We accompanied him to see tables littered with unfinished meals, beds unmade, clothing scattered around in wild disorder. Everything about these houses told of the sudden departure to the harbour for evacuation. Curtains flapped out of open windows and vegetables and flowers stood untended in the garden. What could be done? We just closed the doors and windows and locked up as best we could. The job was too big for small groups of people to do.

Then the Germans were here. We were told not to stand near the windows and not to go outside for fear that we would attract attention. The atmosphere was pregnant with hushed expectancy.

Shopping had to be done, so my mother, Francis and I waited anxiously while bread and milk were obtained. On his return, my father locked up carefully and told us to be quiet. German troops were in the street outside and some doors were being kicked by young louts in uniform demanding that the women should polish their jackboots. This was soon stopped by order of their officers. They wished to treat us better than the rest of Europe, or so it seemed. Some days were to pass before we felt ready to go anywhere near these troops.

Soon we were passing them by with barely a glance. The privates were mainly young and exuberant, the older ones among them more sober and inclined to sightseeing. They seemed to have no idea where they were and names such as Charing Cross intrigued them. I am sure that many of them believed that they were on the English coast and could march to London. An inseparable piece of their equipment seemed to be a soft leather satchel or briefcase, which they used for shopping, as they cleared the shelves in our shops of goods they obviously could not obtain at home in Germany. Everything was paid for with flimsy occupation marks. They went about in small guttural groups shouting and laughing, accompanied, as always, by the unforgettable sound of their jackboots.

Little has been said about the German army jackboot. It was made of heavy leather, with a capless toe and bold stitching at the back; it was blackened and polished to a moderate shine. It leaned awkwardly away from its partner when unoccupied and contributed to the shabby uniform with compressed trouser legs emerging from it when in use. Short leather straps projected from both sides of each top and were used to pull the boots on. But the thing that was most appealing to their owner was the sole. It was covered with round, flat-topped, steel studs and steel horseshoe heel protectors. No doubt the steel shod boots did not wear quickly, but this economic consideration was not the source of joy to the wearer. It was the noise. The Germans loved their crashing, sliding boots, which made every step a matter of consequence. Even while standing talking they would move their feet, shuffle and stamp to accentuate their speech. When they marched, the rhythm of the unit was marked out by the crash of their jackboots. They loved it.

On one occasion, when we had been occupied for some time, a detachment of about thirty soldiers assembled in the road outside their billet near the Grosvenor Hotel. They usually formed up in about five rows facing the opposite pavement and as soon as their corporal was satisfied, wheeled to face left and marched off. As so often happened, the corporal, taking the time from the marching boots, shouted out, "Ein" and after a moments pause, "Vier". The Unit began to sing lustily, "Ai, ye, ai, yo, ai, yah". The boots crashed, the men sang on and so they continued along Havre-des-Pas and turned up St Clements Road towards Howard Davis Park. "Ai, ye, ai, yo, ai, yah," crash, crash, crash on they went.

A very attractive young girl was tending her pony in a stable that gave on to the bottom of St Clement's Road. The approaching martial noise, although pleasing to the trained Germanic ear, irritated her to distraction and as the unit passed, she tossed a full shovel of good, fresh stable muck right over them. There was consternation, the disciplined unit dissolved into a shambles of men trying to wipe the foul mud off their faces and uniforms. Soon the girl was arrested and marched off in the middle of the now silent men, still wearing her riding gear.

But that was not the end of it. She was eventually put into the prison in Newgate Street, but a visitor arrived in the form of Valerie Le Couteur, an even younger girlfriend who, upon being denied access to the prison, climbed the high, granite prison wall topped with broken glass to say "Hello" to her friend. What could the Germans make of these people?

Snowhill has not changed much. Even today I can see the German soldiers slipping and sliding as they tried to negotiate the sloping granite pavement leading into King Street. The soles of their steel shod boots failing to achieve any grip on the polished surface. They often landed on their bottoms with loud Germanic cursing while their friends roared with laughter. The younger soldiers knew the trap and ran at the slope and slid down with yells of enjoyment as they continued across the road in a final flourish, towards 'Boots' the chemist, with much stamping of boots.

One of the things about the German soldier I have never heard referred to, was their smell; I mean the peculiar odour that hung around them. I am sure that what I am about to write, will raise memories in the minds of those who had duties, which brought them into close contact with the enemy.

The smell was a distinctive mixture of the lubricants and polish used on their equipment, a sort of dubbin on their leather 'Got Mit Uns' belts and jackboots and Cologne. Eau de Cologne I suppose.

The result was this unmistakable, unforgettable odour which pervaded their billets and their very presence. Even when we, as boys, invaded their billets in Green Street barracks looking for food and other 'finds', while they were away on route marches, we could detect the aroma of the German soldier lingering in their rooms.

It did not take the Germans long to establish their presence everywhere. Machinegun posts were set up, with sandbags initially, barbed wire was strung across the roads and promenade railings, and military signs appeared, sometimes painted directly onto the walls. The 'Evening Post' changed its character under German direction and often had a whole page devoted to some 'order' from the Kommandant in English and in German. They even looked Germanic in their style with bold borders around them and, of course, we were ordered to ride our bicycles on the right-hand side of the road.

The keep right rule was sometimes arrogantly ignored by the Germans. I was nearly seriously injured on one occasion. It happened in Beresford Street just as I approached the Victoria Club from Halkett Place. I was riding on the right when a

German Officer drove into Beresford Street from Bath Street in a commandeered British car. He drove quickly towards me. I was in full view and he deliberately drove straight at me. I could not stop in time, or otherwise avoid him, for I was travelling at a good speed and he was coming quickly at me. Although the pavement on my right was high, three or four inches at least, I turned towards it and bumped violently over it towards the steps of the Victoria Club just as his bumper and mudguard brushed past me.

Two large, black lamps graced the steps, one on each side, set on top of a stone balustrade. The lamp bases are still there today. I stood up on my pedals, let go of the handlebars and grabbed the left-hand lamp around its column as my cycle hit the balustrade and ricocheted off, sliding down the pavement. The 'officer' parked his car and strutted past me into the Club without a word as, shaken and not a little bruised, I slid to the pavement. How could anyone do that to a young boy? He could have killed me.

So the occupation began, days of boredom, days of excitement, days of fear, days of hunger. but we were always sure that somehow 'we' would win in the end.

The Jackboot

You are English schoolboys?

Chapter Two   **SWEETS TO SCHOOL**

"Kommen sie hier", the voice, loud and rough, fitted its owner, a sergeant. He was dressed in white fatigue jacket and trousers, not the usual Wermacht field grey. They did nothing to hide his thickset body. A field grey forage cap, edged like his epaulettes with silver braid, spread out over his broad head, in an attempt to reach his ears and failed. Black leather gloves matched his leather belt, holster and jackboots like fashion accessories. "Kommen sie hier", it was uttered with authority.

Francis and I were on our way to school walking up Green Street from the hotel and had just turned into the road from Havre-des-Pas and were now opposite the old British army barracks which then stood at the sea end of Green Street. This was our first excursion to school since the Occupation had started. Word had come to us that the schools were open and we were on our way at 8 o'clock on a fine, summer morning.

School uniform in 1940 was a colourful blazer with a crest on the breast pocket. A pair of grey short trousers gave way to knee length socks circled at the top with colour. A colourful tie lit up the grey shirt and on top we balanced a peaked school cap similarly banded with colour. On our backs swayed a leather satchel secured firmly to our shoulders by two leather straps. The German sergeant had never seen anything like it before, not in Poland, not in Belgium and certainly not in France this spring.

"Kommen sie hier". We crossed the road from our pavement to his side where he stood behind the low granite wall, which formed the boundary between the barrack yard and the pavement. Behind his bulging figure stood his men at attention in two rows, rifles gripped firmly at their sides and eyes fixed on a point somewhere on the higher granite wall which lined the pavement we had just abandoned. Behind them stood the once friendly, brick barracks with their iron railings along the first floor, external walkway with red painted fire buckets left by our own soldiers,

"You are English schoolboys?" He demanded, now so close to us that every detail of his uniform and face was crystallised in our minds. We could hardly deny the offence, so we gulped, nodded and admitted it. He was pleased with himself, his men were sure to admire his skill and ease with English. "Gut", he said in his guttural accent. Then, unsure what to say next, he nodded heavily and tried "Gut" again and began reaching into his upper right breast pocket, which was surmounted by the Wermacht eagle with the Nazi swastika between its talons. He had difficulty with that small, grey, metal button finished with a patterned surface like tiny punch marks. His gloves did not help, but he did not remove them.

Francis and I suspected that something awful was about to happen. My senses were heightened and I remember smelling the scent of the leaves on the trees which stood near us and through their flickering light saw the dust slowly settling from the army drill which had been halted for our benefit.

Slowly, or so it seemed, a silver tube was drawn from his pocket. It was a Rowntree's Fruit Gum packet fresh from the shelf of some local sweet shop. His thick, gloved fingers rustled with the silver paper and he looked at us. "Hold out your hand", he ordered. I imagined that he was going to put a fruit gum into his own mouth to savour better the moment as he tormented us. We had heard all about the German soldiers and their ways since the war had started only a few months ago.

"Here", he said moving to place a sweet in Francis' right hand. "No thank you, Sir", said Francis, well-trained not to accept sweets from strangers. "Nein, take", said our new 'friend' and pushed a gum into Francis' hand and then into mine.

He breathed heavily and began to put his sweets back into his uniform pocket. We transferred our sweets from our right to our left hand and raised our caps in unison, me taking my cue and time from my older brother. "Thank you very much Sir", we chimed and almost turned to leave. "Nein", he said, almost gently, "eat, is gut!" We placed the sweets in our mouths, realising that these would probably be poisoned or drugged, whatever, by this very action we were betraying everything British.

"Is gut?" We nodded. "Go to school", he said slowly, fondly patting my head with a gloved paw, "Go to school." We turned and left, not too hurriedly, but in that apprehensive way that one would leave the presence of a raging dog held by an irresponsible boy on a weak lead. Just as soon as we were out of sight we took the unsucked sweets out of our mouths and threw them down a drain and spat out any remaining flavour too. It had been a near thing.

This was our first encounter with the occupying force and was destined not to be our last. I imagine now, looking back, that he may well have had two boys like us in Germany and wanted to speak to us through feelings of homesickness, after all, he was nearly a thousand miles from home.

We dismantle a Chapel

Chapter Three WE DISMANTLE A CHAPEL

The German Hauptman was looking up at the old corrugated iron chapel at the back of the Marina Hotel along the boundary, which formed the road. Gloved hands on hips, he moved a step this way and that as he surveyed the Victorian building in its green paint and chapel windows. At a respectful distance stood a sergeant waiting for his officer to make up his mind. My father saw them from inside the kitchen, which joined the chapel, the sole remnant of the old aquarium, which he had converted to a hotel and restaurant in 1936.

The appearance of this pair was our first real contact with the occupying force and we could guess that they were considering taking over the chapel for some military purpose, possibly as a drill hall and instruction centre. Once they commandeered this, it would not be long before they would take the hotel too. All the other hotels on each side of us had been taken, the La Plage, the Fort D'Auvergne and the Ommaroo.

"Good morning", my father was determined not to seem anxious, although he must have been. The officer did not reply, but kept on looking. At length he said, "You are the owner of this building?" This agreed, he demanded to see the interior and strutted round, his riding boots squeaking slightly. He removed his gloves and began to look upwards at the high roof and at the wooden lining as though this was all terribly important. His right hand holding the gloves began to tap his left hand with them. "So, he said, I will come back," clicked his heels slightly and left with his sergeant. He would not return for a few days. "He's going to get permission to commandeer this building", my father told us.

The following morning, Francis and I were surprised to see my father busy on the roof of the chapel undoing the thick screwnails with large lead washers that secured the corrugated iron. One by one the sheets slid to the ground. We were soon helping. Within a short time the bare roof beams stood exposed to the midday sun. We removed the pine linings with a will and the following day the corrugated walls were disappearing too. By the end of the fourth day the job was done and all that was left of the chapel was a pile or two of neatly stacked timber and several smaller stacks of corrugated iron. A cement path led down one side, terminating in a vestibule which gave on to the street through a glazed, panelled door. We awaited the return of the Hauptman with some trepidation.

A week or so later he reappeared with the same sergeant. It is difficult to describe his face and manner; to say he was agitated is true, but he was also apoplectic, speechless and looking quite ridiculous. The little English at his command failed him, so he resorted to loud German. My father would not let us come near, so we had contented ourselves, my mother, Francis and me, with a distant vantage point. My father was smiling and waving his arms in generous round gestures towards the building saying such things as, "Building coming down. No good, no good," and proffering pieces of rotten timber which he had preserved for this purpose.

It took the German several minutes to calm down and at one time, early on in the 'conversation,' we thought he was going to draw his pistol from its pigskin holster over his left hip. At last he left, yelling abuse and not cutting a very elegant figure. His face was red and he was beside himself with rage. The sergeant tripped dutifully after him. We wondered if we had seen the last of them. To our surprise, my father immediately turned to and began to erect a timber frame for a corrugated iron fence along the road. The sheets were about seven feet long and with plenty of good materials and our help he soon had a sturdy fence in place. That fence was to stand throughout the Occupation and surely saved us from many intrusions by the German army, but not all, for two calamitous visits were yet to be made.

'Billy's Lido 1942
Where have all the dancers gone?

Chapter Four   BILLY'S LIDO

It must have been considered 'quite modern' in the '30's to build an open-air dance floor on the seafront at Havre-des-Pas and yet that was Billy's Lido. The level, concrete dance floor was finely finished to allow for the sliding footwork of the fox-trot and the unrestrained abandon of the Charleston. The surface was inlaid with broad geometric bands of red and blue set off against an off-white background of the floor itself. A neat angular building panelled with steel, Critall french windows on the sides facing the dance floor, occupied the corner nearest to the Marina Hotel from which it was separated by a strip of waste ground. The cement faced, flat roofed building was itself in the '30's' style and provided a covered area for a small indoor dance floor, some seating, a small bar and, of course the band. A low perimeter wall surrounded the whole area and just off the road was a small car park. Strings of bright coloured lights gave an attractive atmosphere.

To a nine-year-old boy, the effect was magical. Add to this the holidaymakers in good numbers dancing to the Lambeth Walk, the sound of the waves drawing on the pebbles beneath the adjoining promenade and sea wall and it was outside my experience of life in conservative Edinburgh. I was to recall this scene many times with deep nostalgia as I played on Billy's Lido or passed it by during the dark days that were to follow. The gaiety of 1939 made the grim darkness of the ensuing '40's even more sombre.

It must have been in the spring of 1941 when I was passing Billy's Lido, and the Germans had by this time become an established and accepted part of life. The La Plage Hotel, which adjoined Billy's Lido, was full of young front-line troops who occupied it as their barrack. Boisterous, yelling and laughing loudly and delighting in the harsh sound of their metal -shod jackboots on the granite pavements.

A machinegun unit was practising clearing stoppages in their MG-42 'Spandau' light machinegun. Under the watchful eye of an Unteroffizier, two soldiers at a time would slam to the ground alongside the gun and load a short belt of blank ammunition with one, dummy, black plastic cartridge in the belt. A short burst was fired, a 'jam' and in a moment the hinged cover to the action was thrown forward, the large, black butt twisted through ninety degrees and pulled back to disgorge a long, blue-black coil spring gleaming with oil. The belt was lifted and dropped past the misfire, the jam was cleared and the 'Spandau' reassembled finishing with another short burst of fire.

I was fascinated. These men were doing this against a stopwatch as though playing a game, laughing and cheering in a disciplined way. I stood in the car park and watched. The smell of burnt powder and drifting blue smoke, the skill of the 'game', held me spellbound. This was Billy's Lido in 1941.

Then a young German officer sauntered by on the promenade, a Lieutenant with the iron cross and wearing the normal uniform jacket with peaked cap and riding boots. He hesitated and watched with a broad smile as the units now 'performed' while the officer was watching. I could see that they were fairly bursting with pride as they took their turns. A more earnest mood settled over them. The rate of clearing increased.

Suddenly a young soldier jumped to his feet from where he was squatting with the others and came rigidly to attention. The N.C.O. growled a question and with eyes fixed on some distant point, the young soldier made his request. The Unteroffizier replied and marched over to the Lieutenant and saluted. I could not hear their voices, but the officer stepped up onto one of the promenade benches, so recently occupied by British holidaymakers and over the wall onto the Lido floor. Standing near the gun, he nonchalantly removed his cap and then his jacket.

He moved to position behind the machinegun and the N.C.O. moved to the left position. At a word from one of the soldiers, now holding the stopwatch, one of the men produced a black band of material and blindfolded the young officer then stood smartly back. The stopwatch clicked as a command was barked and officer and N.C.O. fell to work as one. The mechanism and butt flew and when the pair stood up to attention at the end of their drill, a time was shouted and the detachment broke into a cheer.

Obviously, this was some crack machinegunner, probably promoted from the ranks where he was known for his prowess with the 'Spandau'. Was this really Billy's Lido? Where were the carefree dancers and the little band now? One of the soldiers turned and caught my eye, reaching down he picked up an empty cartridge case and threw it to me with a grin. It was warm from lying in the sun and had about the acrid smell of burnt powder and hot oil.

This was not to be my only engraved memory of Billy's Lido. When my father had purchased the Aquarium building, which was to be the Marina Hotel, he had embarked with vigour on a development project, which had ended abruptly at the outset of war. Architect's plans still showed a new entrance foyer and kitchens yet to be built. How he found all the materials, such as cement, I do not know, but I believe some of the German fortifications may have been short of a bag or two. Somehow he began to build, at first the extended kitchen, then the foyer and office in the new entrance.

A young Jerseyman with Canadian accent helped him, he was Basil De Guelle. Mr. Jean was a fine old gentleman who lived across the road with his sister. Mr Jean was intriguing, he had written a book in manuscript form about the foreshore life on the beaches and rocks of Havre-des- Pas. It was beautifully illustrated with his own watercolours of many sea creatures such as squid. He was also a skilled and sensitive photographer and a master plumber. It was the latter gift, which particularly attracted my father, and Mr Jean was soon cheerfully employed plumbing the hotel.

A good friend was found in Louis Ollivro who lived with his wife, a very pretty girl, at Pontac. Louis was very interested in making battery cells out of jam jars, strips of copper and 'bluestone'. Each cell produced one volt and it took ninety cells, a formidable array, to power Louis's battery radio! As a lorry driver, he had been required by the Germans to do such work as they required from time to time and I am sure that this was the source of much building material. However, one material was very difficult to 'find' and that was roofing felt. Do you remember the little Bar and bandstand in the corner of Billy's Lido? Through the windows, now very dirty with disuse, we had seen many rolls of roofing felt belonging to our conquerors.

Late one evening, the three of us dropped over the wall adjoining the wasteland next to the bandstand and crawling through the long grass, found a narrow metal window.

The window soon gave way to a little persuasion and we were busy handing out the required rolls of felt, when suddenly we saw the regular patrol of two sentries walking side by side towards Mount Bingham. They were deep in conversation and we could hear the murmur of their voices. We dropped to the ground and when they had passed continued with our exploit.

When the 'Gestapo' raided our Hotel, they searched and found radios and other things, but all around them were building materials in the form of rooms and a roof which they never 'saw'.

Gingerpop!

Chapter Five   **GINGERPOP AND SCHNAPPS**

Gingerpop was an old-fashioned drink, a ginger flavoured lemonade, tawny in colour, but with a distinct white head. This described the tomcat which came into our lives in 1940 and which stayed with us throughout the war. He adopted us, we had no say in the matter and began immediately to stamp his personality on all his dealings with the family. To say that he was a character just begins to describe this tough, affectionate, wiry, relaxed, adventurous, loveable cat. I believe that his presence in our midst did much to make a life, which could be tedious, more bearable.

Let me start with his arrival. He belonged, if this cat could ever have belonged, to the shopkeeper's family across the road from the Marina, the Sohiers. His decision to cross the road permanently was quite irrevocable and much in character with his way of doing things; he arrived in July 1940, settled in and that was that. We found ourselves possessed of a large tom, who was immediately christened Gingerpop.

At first feeding our lodger was no problem, as with many other households we had plenty of scraps and could still buy fish, but as things became tighter, fish disappeared from the market and we used every scrap of food we had. Gingerpop knew that he was onto a good thing and that we would not let him down. His best stroke of luck came when we found an overlooked tin of Salmon and Shrimp paste, weighing about two pounds, in a kitchen cupboard. The tin was rusty, but appeared to be airtight. On opening it my father decided that we should not eat it, but by general agreement a small portion was offered to Gingerpop who gave it a definite claws up and devoured this tasty treat. By dint of careful management this tin was eked out over days until he had licked his lips on the last tasty morsel.

Searching round for something else to feed our cat, my mother struck upon limpets. We had heard that they were good eating and that the old Jersey folk used to eat them quite regularly. Our source of much of this information was Mr Jean who lived with his sister at 'Bayview' and who had compiled the book with beautiful illustrations on the shore life at Havre-des-Pas.

My mother asked Francis and me to gather some limpets from the rocks in front of the Hotel. Armed with hammers and a container we set off in pursuit of our quarry only to discover that we had taken a hammer to crack a limpet when only stealth and cunning will move them without crushing them to a useless pulp. To remove a limpet from a rock, we soon learned, you have to approach from downwind exercising extreme caution, the least sense of your presence sending them into an iron grip of their rock face which defied every effort to prise them free.

Returning with our limpets, we saw them cooked on the AGA and a transformation in Gingerpop who began to patrol the area of the kitchen nearest the cooker. The cooked limpets were spread out to cool on the draining board and we witnessed for the first time Gingerpop's limpet routine. The draining board was too high for him to see onto from the floor and he did not wish to jump up onto it. Instead, he just stood up at full stretch and reached up and over with his paw until he felt a limpet which he then pulled down to eat it eagerly on the floor. We never had to worry about food for him again.

Trots, that is static fishing lines baited with several hooks at intervals along their length, were often used on the beach among the rocks of the 'Three Sisters'. These worked quite well and yielded some good fish. Gingerpop discovered this rich source of his favourite food and could be seen at half-tide trotting down to the wet beach, looking neither to right nor to left, but heading straight for the trot.

Having secured his fish, the journey up the beach was no easy matter, for he would not eat the prize where he had 'found' it, but dragged it and carried it several hundred feet. The gulls were swift to spot him and came in to drive him off his fish. Flying low they would screech at him and dive bomb, before breaking away at zero altitude. Gingerpop's response was to drop his fish and bat at the gulls with his paws fearlessly and then to continue the journey to his lair.

Mention of Gingerpop's name and its association with a soft drink has reminded me of an occasion in Roseville Street when I was walking up towards Colomberie. I noticed a fine mural, which had been painted by a German soldier on the wall of what had been a long, narrow garage on the left side of the street. I stood looking at it for a few moments. It showed a team of German army horses pulling a gun and limber along a muddy road and the soldiers riding on the limber and on one of the horses were smartly turned out in idealised uniforms with faces filled with pride. The mural must have been six feet high and twenty feet long and was well executed in oils even if the subject was not to my taste.

An 88mm anti-tank gun had been pulled out of the garage and a very young German soldier was cleaning and oiling its mechanism. He had taken off his shirt and his identification tags flew around his neck as he worked. As I passed him he looked up from his work and then straightened up. In his right hand he held a two inch wide clear plastic tube with a cork firmly fixed in one end while the other end was flattened to permit a felt wick of about two inches wide to emerge. The bottle was filled with golden coloured oil. He raised the oil bottle to his lips tilted it back in a drinking motion and lowering it, smiled at me, "Schnapps" he said. I am sure that his sergeant would have given him Schnapps if he had seen him idling from his work.

Gingerpop was not the only animal on the beach. The Bartlett family who lived opposite the Fort D'Auvergne Hotel had an Alsatian dog and it was this dog that performed one of those episodes, which can hardly be explained. The German soldiers often spent their off-duty hours on the beach in front of the hotels and they were no different really from the holidaymakers of the 1930's. They wore a variety of swimming trunks or boxer shorts and soon developed a healthy tan. They used quantities of sunning oils and their bodies glistened in the sun. The accompanying aroma wafted off their hot skins, was unusual, but otherwise they were perfectly normal.

They played games, laughed and shouted, swam vigorously or sedately in the sea and obviously enjoyed their war. At other times they sat and chatted, resting their backs against the warm granite of the sea wall. They sometimes read 'Die Signal', full of photographs, rather like a thin version of 'The Picture Post', but carrying advertisements for 'Stalheims', the well-known German coal scuttle helmet, which patriotic Germans obviously bought. A favourite spot to sit was along the cement and granite slab at the foot of the sea wall just beneath the Fort D'Auvernge. Several young Germans were swinging their feet in the rising tide when our patriotic Alsatian hove into view.

Ignoring these members of the superior race, he hurried along the paved slab just behind them carelessly brushing his fur and tail against their backs. Suddenly he stopped and retraced his steps to carefully sniff at one of the backs, a quick decision followed and in the way of dogs, he swung around and cocked up his right back leg and proceeded to do what dogs normally do when in this position. At first the German did not react, a pleasant warm sensation must have coursed down his spine, without looking, he put his hand behind him and came into direct contact with the offending dog. What a shout went up, followed by diving straight into the shallow sea and splashing about with much swearing accompanied by hysterical laughter from his 'kamaraden'.

The Alsatian strolled off quite unconcerned. Towards the end of the occupation, when food supplies had dwindled to nothing and the Germans were gathering nettles to make their Goulash, cats began to disappear and dogs too. The German technique was to catch a cat and put it immediately into a sack, which they then hit against a wall. Gingerpop evaded all attempts to capture him. He never trusted the Germans from the first and always made off at their approach. I am sure that he would have been too tough to eat. If he did decide to stay indoors it was to lie full length on top of a tall cupboard in the kitchen from which vantage point he could survey the room.

Early on in the war, we had acquired a bread slicer, which had a fixed blade and slid back and forward in a wooden frame when worked by hand. It was important to us, because it cut up our ration into neat slices and avoided the slightest waste. It was a source of great delight to Gingerpop who would jump down from his lofty perch and play Russian roulette with the moving blade to obtain the odd crust of bread. He was never in the slightest danger so swift was the movement of that dextrous paw.

When the Liberation of Jersey took place, Gingerpop shared in our joy and of our table, now well provided with titbits of interest to a sophisticated cat. A year passed and we prepared to leave the Island and the problem of Gingerpop loomed over our affairs. However, the new owners of the Marina agreed to take him on and we were happy enough. On returning to Jersey nearly a year later we called in to the Hotel to see Gingerpop only to learn that he had pined for us and had died some weeks after our departure. A sad end to a good tom who had seen us through the war.

Nature claims a German Bunker - La Collette

Chapter Six   LA COLLETTE

Not far from Havre-des-Pas, towards the harbour, and approached by a delightful promenade, was our happy hunting ground, the area known as La Collette. Francis and I often went there and spent many hours fishing, without much luck as I recall, although Francis did catch a beautiful mullet on one occasion with primitive tackle of the bent pin variety which must have caused one or two of the better prepared fishermen to consider suicide. We fished from the remains of the old breakwater which had once been part of a grandiose Victorian scheme to enclose a large deepwater harbour with this arm which was to reach out to the finished arm, the breakwater of Elizabeth Castle. Storms and high seas had brought the bold Victorian engineers' plan to nought, with huge cement blocks being easily displaced by equally large waves. The Germans did not learn from this example, although the evidence was all around for them to see.

It occurred to the Fortress planners that a strong pillbox of massive proportions would be well sited to see off the attacking Tommies if it was built on the standing part of La Collette breakwater. Francis and I witnessed at very close quarters the lengthy preparations required for this bastion to survive a sustained attack, including heavy shellfire and bombing. Unfortunately the German engineers did not also consider the effect of the gently lapping water at their feet.

Drilling the tough concrete of the old breakwater took many hours, for the holes were numerous and deep, drilled in a regular pattern to accept steel reinforcing bars set in concrete. Summer days passed and we climbed onto the breakwater over the rocks from Havre-des-Pas, scarcely attracting any attention from the Org Todt squads of builders. Gradually a huge web of interlaced steel formed the structure with barely room to pass a football between the geometrically precise steel rods. Arc welders continuously flashed and sparked and men crawled within, like elements in a modern sculpture. Winter came at last and with it large wooden boards securely fastened to the lower part ready for infilling with concrete. It would soon be finished and the men could move on to other work to make the Fortress secure. They must have been very proud of this monument which stood foursquare with no attempt at concealment.

The gale, when it came, was severe and lasted for a few days. The waves rolled in from the South and threw their spray high up above the breakwater as though flexing their muscles ready to show what they could do. One dark, stormy morning we looked out from the Marina Hotel to see the breakwater supporting a drunken mass of twisted and bent steel where once had stood the symbol of German power. Francis and I battled against the wind along the little promenade to gaze from the shelter of the granite cliff through the salt-laden spray to see the ruins of this huge undertaking. The white foam just poured through the twisted structure causing it to move and we could feel the enormous thud of the waves breaking against the breakwater. We did not feel at all sad for the Germans, but rather elated at their defeat by the sea.

Later, as we visited the area, we were to see the Germans slowly cut up the useless wreckage and start again on the bunker, which still stands there today.

Francis and I still laugh at my father's attempts to get us home on time for lunch or tea. We did not mean to be disobedient, but time meant nothing to us when we fished or explored this exciting area, now so sadly lost to development. You see we had no watches and therefore no idea of the time and there was so much to do. At last, in desperation, just as we were setting off one morning armed with our fishing gear, my father appeared with an alarm clock, which he proceeded to tie securely to my middle as it would not fit into my pocket. It was set to go off at the appropriate hour when we should return and it was of the old type with prominent twin bells at the top.

I looked and felt like a pregnant duck. Francis could hardly walk or speak for laughing at me and if any German had opened my coat he would have thought that I was a bomb waiting to go off. I think it worked, but I do not remember wearing it again.

At the shore end of the breakwater there was an odd little wall, very thick and made of concrete, about six feet high. It must have been part of the Victorian strategy in the early days of building their breakwater. Behind this stood several items of interest for which the Germans had no use. Denuded of their painted canvas lay four wings of a De Havilland Rapide brought down from the airport, the craftsmanship of their construction was a delight to see and I managed to obtain one small wingtip section from the decaying remains.

Alongside the wings stood several cars towed round from the pier after being abandoned there by their owners during the evacuation. One close-coupled Humber saloon always brought back memories as I looked at it at various times during the Occupation. I could see it standing there on the pier with crowds milling round it as they made their way to the ships. Some of the ships were only coal vessels and quite unsuited for the evacuation, but if you wanted to go that was what was available.

I stood with my father and Francis on one side as cars swept onto the pier on that deceptively charming morning in 1940.

The drivers did not even attempt to park, they just stopped, doors flew open and people just struggled out with cases and parcels and made off to orderly queues without closing the car doors, or in some cases even switching off the ignition. It was strange and disconcerting to watch. After a while we walked away towards the town, but had not gone far when a very new Standard Flying Sixteen drew up alongside us. This 1939 model gleamed in its maroon paint work and was a very pretty car in its day. The driver leaned over to open the front passenger door and asked my father if we would like a lift to wherever we were going. He was a youngish man dressed in a smart pinstripe suit and could have been a bank clerk. At first my father declined his offer, but the young man persisted and to tell the truth it was a very odd time to live through with ordinary human contacts performing somersaults. So Francis and I found ourselves sitting in the back of this delightful car while its driver took us to Havre-des-Pas.

"How do you like this car?" our excited chauffeur asked. We told him that it was very nice. This unleashed a stream of conversation, which in normal times would have been quite unexpected. It appeared that our friend had just been given the car by its owner, who had driven it to the pier with his wife and was now boarding a boat for England and did not know when he would return, if ever. But this was not all, the farmer, for that is what he was, had also given the young man his farm to look after for the duration of the war. Little wonder he was so excited.

The old Humber was just one of these abandoned cars, yet so full of memories. I casually let down the luggage platform from its narrow boot and felt how unusually heavy it was. Noticing two flush catches along its edge, I undid them to find that this was a lid revealing a fitted set of tools now rusting quietly as the war went on.

I imagine that every time I visited this area I always found
something new to examine or to observe, shells both natural
and manmade were not uncommon. Some boys I knew by sight
found a complete light calibre shell washed up on the beach
between the swimming pool at Havre-des-Pas and the Dicq at
Greve d'Azette. They stood around in a small group giving
advice, while one of their number attempted to remove the fuse.
The shell exploded and one boy was killed and the others
seriously injured.They were dangerous times to be young and
inquisitive.

That shell may have come from one of the wrecks which began
to litter the South coast of the island. Some wrecks were as the
result of natural forces and others resulted from attacks on
shipping near the islands usually from the air. The 'Mazagan'
was a barge and came towards Jersey from the South in the
early winter of 1942, either bad navigation or a failure of her
gear saw her driven onto the rocks just to the east of the Demi-
des-Pas light. She lay wallowing for some time before being
broken up by the sea.

Before she disappeared, Francis and 'Dicky' Williams decided
that a visit would be worthwhile. For the purpose they chose a
beach catamaran or float of about eight feet in length and
paddled off from the back of the swimming pool at half-tide. It
was hard paddling between the rocks and amid the rush of water
through the gullies, but the intrepid pair, without a thought for
the Germans, at last made it to the wreck. The wash of seas
over the partly submerged hull made boarding difficult, but they
achieved this and secured their little craft on deck.

A search revealed cases of ruined oranges soaked and pulped in seawater and fat, distorted packs of French butter covered in seaweed and oil. However, all was not lost, a case yielded to their touch and out came a square bottle with Cointreau written on its label. Now neither Francis nor 'Dicky' was accustomed to strong drink at their tender age and neither did they know what Cointreau was. Rising to the occasion, 'Dicky', a year older than Francis said, "This is what you do to get into these".

Suiting the action to the words he knocked off the top off the bottle and poured some of the clear liquid into his mouth, handing the bottle to Francis with a too rapid movement of his arm. Francis followed suit to find himself, like his friend quite speechless as the liquid poured down his throat. They managed to secure a few items aboard their float and with a glowing feeling of well-being made their way back to the 'Pool' where they divided their spoils and made their happy way home.

I wonder if pieces of the 'Mazagan' are still there today?

The High Court Judge

Chapter Seven   **THE HIGH COURT JUDGE**

I suppose he was really my mother's friend, but both my parents liked him very much from the first moment of their initial meeting. His name was Ferris, perhaps it was Ferrers, I was never sure how it was spelt, he was very tall indeed and well built. His hair was his outstanding feature, it was as white as it could be and it grew in barely controlled confusion above a rather proud, arrogant face. As though aware that his head was a living bust to a man of greatness, he habitually wore a long black, cloak which concentrated attention on the upper part of his fine figure. I was twelve and very impressed, he must have been in his sixties.

My mother had a natural ability to get on with people and was an extrovert compared with my father. An Edinburgh civil servant when she met my father by dint of driving her open Morris Cowley into his motorworks for petrol, she had returned more than once to fill up again. I suspect that she had her car's tank drained elsewhere. She was a complete contrast to Grant Ferris, she was short, with raven black straight hair which she kept carefully and wore with a fringe. Born on Achill Island on the West Coast of Ireland, she claimed links with the native Irish aristocracy, the O'Mally's. Also with a twinkle in her eye, links with one of the Spanish Armada who had struggled ashore when his ship was wrecked along with many others on that Atlantic coast. The Kilcoyne family, for that was her maiden name, had moved to Edinburgh in the late 1800's and her father had become a senior official in the Edinburgh Water Board enjoying visits of inspection by chauffeur driven car to the various reservoirs which surrounded the City.

They met Mr Ferris one Sunday outside our church and struck up a lasting friendship. We soon learnt that Mr Ferris had come to Jersey in the 1930's to acclimatise himself after years of service in India as a High Court judge. He was living with his wife at the Ommaroo Hotel, where they had a suite. Many other expatriates lived in a similar manner in Jersey. It was a popular destination for them because of its climate, scenery and low cost accommodation. At first Mr Ferris came alone to enjoy tea, such as it was at that time, and a long conversation. He gradually explained that his wife was in poor health, suffering from an illness she had contracted while in India. My mother and Mrs Ferris met at the Ommaroo Hotel and became close friends, spending many afternoons in each other's company. Little did they know how important to Mr and Mrs Ferris this friendship was to become.

It was a lovely summer afternoon and Mrs Ferris had decided to sit in the main entrance of their Hotel to enjoy the sunlight and the view. She never gave a thought to the diamond, sapphire and ruby brooch shaped in the form of a RAF's pilot's wings when she pinned it onto her blouse. Her son, who was serving in the RAF, had given it to her when he had flown solo for the first time. Strangely, the Germans had permitted several English people like the Ferris's to retain rooms in the Ommaroo, although they had quartered officers in all the others.

The young Luftwaffe pilot had only recently been posted to Jersey and had been allocated a room in the hotel. He had been out and on returning cut quite a dash in his tailored uniform, riding boots and peaked cap. Among the German officers, the Luftwaffe were nearly always the most elegant. He passed Mrs Ferris where she sat in the sunlight, but turned back at once and stood directly in front of her. His face worked with emotion. He bowed curtly and said "Madam, would you please remove that badge, it is offensive to the German forces."

At first Mrs Ferris could not understand what he meant. She was quite frail and not used to being addressed like this by a stranger, but she soon gathered herself together and told the young German that she would not do as he requested. Her son had given her that brooch and she was proud to wear it. As far as she was concerned that, was the end of the matter, but I am afraid this foolish little man was not prepared to let it rest there. Mr Ferris came upon the scene and an altercation followed which he could not win. The Felgendarmerie was called and he was taken for questioning to their headquarters As a result of this he was sentenced to a term of imprisonment, in France I believe, and was given time to gather his clothing before reporting to the harbour.

I first became aware of all this when I found my father obtaining sugar, butter and flour and baking thin shortbread biscuits which he packed carefully into a tubular tin which they fitted exactly. I remember tasting one of these beautiful biscuits. We were told that this was one of the best sources of food and energy and that Mr Ferris would need every one of them where he was going. And so, sadly, he was dragged away from his wife who was distraught.

Some weeks later, my mother arranged for her friend to enter the "The Limes" nursing home in Green Street to be cared for when she became confined to her room. My mother's visits to the nursing home were long and happened every day. Sometimes I would be sent to Mrs Ferris on some mission, usually in the evening. She was very gentle and kind. I enjoyed my visits for quite another reason. There was a lovely young French girl, an ancillary, who loved to chat with me in broken French. We used to sit in a little office for half-an-hour or so and she began to keep little treats for me, leftovers from the dinner. I think that this was the first time I realised just how nice girls can be, I have not changed my mind since.

Mrs Ferris soon died, pining for her husband. If anything made me dislike the Nazis it was this one event, but not all Germans were Nazis and from my small experience of them, there were many 'good' Germans who disliked their leaders from Hitler downwards, occasionally we came into contact with one.

Mr Ferris returned after his wife's death, but it was some time later, and if my memory serves me, it was after the Liberation. He was a typical English gentleman of the very best stamp.

You can't be riding your bicycle home in this.

Chapter Eight   GOVERNMENT HOUSE 1942

It was one of the blackest afternoons I remember. In school we had watched the sky become overcast and gradually it became almost as dark as night. When the storm broke the rain cascaded down in torrents as though it would never stop, accompanied by loud peals of thunder and vicious flashes of lightning. I did not look forward to riding my cycle back to Havre-des-Pas, but when the end of school came, that was what faced me. I got my cycle out of the rack and had just reached the top of the driveway, when I saw John Bonhomme about to get into a little car. John was a close friend and the car was a little Austin Seven Ruby saloon of about 1937. It was green and had enormous, black, shiny discs covering its wheels, which were normally spoked and, even in the rain, I could see that it was a beautifully kept little car.

John saw me and spoke quickly to the driver and then gave me a wave to come over. He introduced me to his uncle, Mr Young, who was driving the car. The uncle was a jolly sort of man with a soft accent and a twinkle in his eye. "You can't be riding your bicycle home in this", he said, "would you like to come with John, leave your cycle here and I'll bring you back when the rain stops". I gladly accepted and was soon riding along in style in this elegant little car.

John told me that his uncle was the butler at Government House and we were going there for tea. I knew that Government House was occupied by the island Kommandant and said as much to John, for I was not willing to go there and fraternise with the Germans. However John told me that we would be going to the staff quarters and not upstairs. Mr Young told me as he drove along, that he was from Eire, which was neutral and had been butler to the last British Governor who, on leaving the island, had asked Mr Young to stay on, if at all possible to keep the house in order. The Kommandant had accepted this arrangement with good grace and Mr Young never doubted that he was keeping faith with his last Governor and that the British would return.

On arriving at the house by the back road from St Saviour's church, we were hurried into a large kitchen where Mrs Young reigned as cook. She was lovely, round and soft and gentle, always laughing and glad to see you. A perfect cook, the only other member of staff was a maid, also Irish, thin and quick.

To my surprise hot claret was made and I was given a full glass like everyone else to sip and enjoy. The hot liquid was just right for the stormy conditions outside and the spices soon gave me a sense of warmth and well being, but I still felt guilty about being so close to the Germans, even if they were not in the room.

John and I sat at a big table and chatted and soon we were forgotten while the rain continued to hammer on the glass windows. A door into the kitchen opened and in walked a German officer in his shirtsleeves and braces. He left the door open and walked across the room to fetch something. John nudged me and said, "That's Hans Stuck, the racing driver.' Stuck was well known for his handling of the huge six litre Mercedes racing cars at Donnington and elsewhere in the pre-war European circuit. Boys magazines were full of artist's impressions of the great, Mercedes cars racing against the rear engined Auto Unions, their only serious rival on the circuits.

These silver beasts outperformed our own E.R.A.s and the French and Italian machinery. I must have expressed some surprise, for Stuck turned round and looked straight at us and

smiled, but said nothing while I gazed in boyish wonder at him. He left the kitchen, but soon came back and without a word placed a postcard of himself, one of those artist's impressions tinted in brown, on the table in front of me.
It was signed in a very German hand, Hans Stuck.

Apparently Stuck was aide to the Kommandant, a nice posting for a hero of the Reich, I saw him again in the future when I visited John, who sometimes stayed at Government House with his aunt and uncle, but I never spoke to him. He had commandeered a lovely little Morgan 4/4 drophead in British Racing Green and drove it very smartly. One of his pleasures was to sit in the sunshine on an old chair at the entrance to the coachouse facing the interior with a .22 rifle across his knees. Inside the coachouse he had placed a barrel in clear view of his position with a plank leading to it from some bales of straw near a rat hole. On the barrel was a piece of cheese. As the rats ran across the plank he shot them.

I only saw the Kommandant once and that closer than I expected, or wanted. Playing with John at the back of the house I noticed an S.S. $2^1/2$ litre saloon arrive at the front, we slipped round to see who it was, but the driver had gone inside and the car stood unattended. We decided to have a look inside it. Just as we were taking in the gleaming new interior of this car we heard footsteps coming towards us and turning found the Kommandant, I have to assume it was him for I had never seen him before, standing in front of us. He was in full uniform, but without his cap and he smiled broadly at our interest in his car and said something in good humour like, "British is good, is best". We were a bit overwhelmed by his sudden appearance and made our exit as fast as decently possible, but not before several other ranking German officers had begun to join him.

Mr Young came to the Marina hotel on a few visits after that, always with some little parcel of food and chatted with my parents about Ireland. He was a charming man who had been left in a very awkward position. I am sure that he wished he had taken his wife to England when the opportunity was still available, instead of acting the part of the perfect English butler and staying at his post while others fled. It must have seemed to many that he was giving comfort and support to the Nazis, which was not his intention, he was carrying out his instructions and Government House was left in good order at the end of the Occupation. Sometimes it was a very odd war.

A strange piece of seaweed.

Chapter Nine   **SMITH AND WESSON .45**

The summer of 1942 was hot and long. I often went to the swimming pool at Havre-des-Pas, which was only a short walk from the Marina Hotel. I did not go immediately to the pool itself on this particular day in my holiday, but went down onto the beach as the tide was out. To my surprise, I saw that the 'pool' was also out. It had been drained by opening the sluice gate at the seaward end and now all the stones and seaweed of which the bottom was comprised, glinted in the sunlight in every direction. I was soon stepping from slippery stone to slippery stone with some friends, all of us intrigued to find a fish or something in one of the many pools. We were all quite well apart, calling out to each other from time to time and I was near the plank bridge which separated the deep side of the pool from the, non-paying, shallow or paddling side when I noticed it.

At first it looked like a piece of the broad, belt-like, brown seaweed, but something about its shape held my attention. I reached down and moved it with my hand, concerned lest it should be a stingfish, which was not uncommon. This was heavy. I pulled it out from under the covering weed and into a clearer patch of gravel. It was a holster. I was sure that it was full of pebbles and sand, but as I lifted it I could see a butt and the metal frame of a very big revolver. In an instant, all my friends were around me wanting to know what I had found, to touch it, to hold it. I wrapped it in my towel next to my swimming costume and made my way past young soldiers sunbathing while off duty, many of them in shorts or swimming costumes and giving off heavy scents of oil or suntan lotion from their hot bodies.

My escort of boys and I arrived at the Marina where I found my father busy with something just inside our gate. I uncovered my find and showed it to him while all the boys stood watching to see his reaction and to hear what he would say. I felt quite proud. "I don't know how you could be so stupid." The words fell over me like a bucket of cold water. "If ever you find something as dangerous as this, leave it alone," I heard my father say. I could not believe it. Here was an object to be proud of and my father was telling me off in front of all my friends. I was so ashamed. "Go off and swim and don't bring back anything more like this." he continued. "I'll get rid of it and you boys, don't mention this to anyone".

We trailed back to the beach crestfallen, me more crestfallen than any while my friends began to brag, as boys do, about what their fathers would have done and comparing my father unfavourably to theirs. At the end of a miserable afternoon, I returned to the hotel. Had I heard the last of the revolver? I went into the kitchen somewhat reluctantly. My father gave me a playful push on my shoulder, "Cheer up" he said, "it's cleaned up nicely." I could not understand what he meant until he produced a silver, Smith and Wesson .45 calibre revolver from behind his back.

"Listen to me, Leo," he said, if ever you find anything like that again, don't show it to all your friends. I had to let them think I was throwing it away in case they should tell everyone that I had a gun." He gave me another gentle push and put the gun into my hands. The revolver was now empty of ammunition, my father had seen to that, but it was in perfect condition, having been heavily greased before being dropped into the pool. We imagined that some retired British Army officer had disposed of it for fear that the Germans would find it in his possession. It was of a type issued before and during the First World War and could have seen service in India. The holster was burnt in the AGA as it's stitching was rotten and the leather was saturated with salt. The revolver was hidden in the passageway, which led to the backstairs, just under a painted, glass panel, which covered an alcove of the restaurant nearby.

The only time I saw it again was when my father stuck it into his belt and closed his jacket over it before he got into his car and drove to 'Gestapo' headquarters at Silvertide on May 8th 1945 to ask for the return of his radios and other property.

'Garlustig sind die jagerei!'

Chapter Ten SCHOOL

Francis and I had been attending the Benedictine Preparatory School in Edinburgh when we came down to Jersey for yet another visit in late 1939. With the decision to stay on in Jersey made by my parents, another school had to be found. So it was that we put on a very different uniform from that we were used to and enrolled for De La Salle College or the 'The Beeches' as we grew to know it.

The Headmaster, Brother Edwards, was a rotund, short man, pleasant, but with a somewhat limited grasp of the intricacies of the pronunciation of the English language. He wore the traditional garb of the Christian Brothers, cassock and flapping neck attire, not unlike an advocate of the Royal Court. He always wore a black skullcap which, in moments of great excitement, he would snatch off his head and wave about to make a point. I am sorry to record that both Francis and I gave him several occasions thus to use his headgear.

The staff who had been there before the outbreak of war remained. I found dear Brother Marcel a kind and thoughtful teacher whom I grew to respect. Unfortunately he made rather a favourite out of me and being a 'new boy' to the school, this did not go down well with my classmates who were as good a crowd of boys as you would find anywhere.

'Timmy' O'Regan must have been the wrong side of forty when I entered his class. He was prim to a fault and an excellent teacher. At the end of the school day as the bell sounded for the end of lessons, he would stand up, slide his chair into the kneehole of his desk, slam his book shut, pull open his right-hand desk drawer, place the book precisely inside. Take out a clothes brush and dust off each shoulder and his jacket front, replace the brush, slam the drawer, adjust his tie and say "Put away your books" He never varied this routine.

One day, his 'bete noir', Ronald Ferguson rigged a very long coil spring beneath this overused drawer and we waited with some anxiety as Timmy went through his ritual at 4 o'clock. Reaching the drawer sequence, he was put out of his stride, as his drawer proved difficult to open and seemed to have a will of it's own in closing itself promptly. Timmy rose to the bait and a great tussle followed which was as good as any Charlie Chaplin short. We were all kept in until Ronald was forced to admit that he was the culprit and was punished with a black gym shoe kept especially for that purpose in yet another drawer.

The school was the perfect grapevine for all that was going on in the island as the boys came from every parish. We knew immediately when an aircraft had crashed and exactly where, leaflets were swapped and many incidents were recorded. Together the whole school witnessed a bombing raid on ships in St. Aubin's Bay as this took place during our morning break.

The German authorities decided that all schoolchildren should learn German. A pleasant German nurse appeared in our classroom and, sometimes in uniform, began the 'task' of teaching us to speak her language. I will be the first to acknowledge that she made a gallant attempt, but to many of my class, to learn German was to assist the enemy. So, though the good nurse persevered. I am, afraid it was all too no avail, but I will return to this later.

One of the first calamities to befall the school was early on in the occupation, when the Medical Officer for the island advised all parents to have their children inoculated against, I believe it was chickenpox. Because of the scale of our undernourishment, it was felt that we would succumb to the illness quickly unless inoculated. The inoculations were administered on the left arm at school and boys were advised to wear a red ribbon or armband on that arm, to avoid accidental knocks. Suppurating wounds appeared on the affected arms which, combined with a high temperature, soon emptied the classrooms. On return to school, some of the boys still had dreadful, swollen arms, which were painful to touch. As with some other parents, I am glad to say that my parents did not allow my brother and I to be inoculated.

Without fuel in the island, the school's central heating system could not be used and as autumn turned to winter we shivered in our classrooms and often we were allowed to wear coats and scarves while we worked. At last the Germans supplied their standard, cylindrical steel stoves. These were fitted to any room by taking a pane of glass out of a window, replacing it with a thin sheet of metal in which a hole had been cut to accept the stove's chimney. You could not see the fire. The stove was top loading and had two rows of 25mm diameter holes around them near the base. Why do I tell you all this? Because we suffered interminably as these 'Trifid-like' monstrosities belched smoke into the room and produced little or no heat.

We started off in the morning, wearing coats and watched a gentle miasma of thin blue smoke ascend to the ceiling, an hour later we were crouching low over our desks as, with smarting eyes, we tried to work. Later, a kind teacher would allow his class to escape to the outside air for a few minutes, as the atmosphere in the room became impossible. Any attempt to stoke or to poke the fire from the top access hole was doomed to produce further clouds of smoke and ash. We longed for the spring and the return of the warmth of the sun.

Paper became a problem. As the old stock of thick jotters with their blue covers was exhausted we were required to turn back and use every available blank space in them on which to work. Exercise books were soon unavailable and we brought in odd assortments of paper. Strangely enough, pens, pencils and rulers always seemed plentiful, but the ink was awful stuff, thin and with lots of debris in it.

My favourite recollection of this time is when our teacher, an innocent man, gave us back our parents' old absence or late notes to write on. It must have taken us all of two minutes to recognise the potential of this bonanza. We soon swapped all the notes and with a little careful doctoring achieved one or two 'fireproof' days off school.

Mr O'Shea was an unqualified teacher, taken on for the duration of the war. He had his moments. Using the parlance of today, he was, I can now see, a poor man's James Bond. We worked in silence under his strict but fair discipline. He meted out punishment quite frequently and he meant it. Francis and I and perhaps two other boys had 'acquired' a hand grenade. It was made of china- like material and had a bluish metal disc at one end which we took to be the fuse. Recalling one of Mr O'Shea's reminiscences of his days fighting in Spain in the 1930's, among his too many other adventures, we sought his advice and guidance.

So, anxious to insert ourselves in to his good books, we sidled up to him when all the other boys had left the class at four o'clock and, producing the hand grenade, asked him to explain it to us! I have never since seen such an impressive reaction. He became agitated to the point of incoherence as we explained what it was and, handling it like a red hot coal, handed it back and may have said, "Get rid of it".

Looking back, it was good advice. We should never have brought it to school, that is obvious, but you can hardly understand the times in which we lived from the viewpoint of today and to us, this was just exciting and ordinary. However, boys were injured and sometimes killed for no more cause than that they were too inquisitive.

I used to cycle or walk home for lunch every day. We had no makings for sandwiches such as ham or butter. My mother kept us going on soups and stews and 'butter' taken off the top of the milk by heating it on our dear old Aga. Boys from farms had no such shortages and I often watched enviously as they ate their sandwiches with thick butter and slices of meat. I used to dream of sandwiches and soft filled rolls. One day I felt quite weak and could hardly make a tight fist, my mother took me to see Doctor Gow and after examining me he issued a voucher for one thin slab of Chocolate Menier cooking chocolate. He told us, with regret, that it was all that he could do. I could hardly eat it knowing that my parents and Francis had none, so I would not eat it until they all had a little. I wished that I had never been given it. The Red Cross parcels made a huge difference to us all.

I had four seasons of rugby in Scotland where we began to play at school from six years old. My class was playing with an old rubber football one afternoon at break time. We were all on the lower pitch, when one of the senior boys from the upper playground came running down, swept up our football and carried it off towards his friends on the higher ground. I never even thought about it, it was so natural, so instinctive that I just took off after him. He was not worried, he knew that he could soon deal with me when I caught up with him. I was nearly alongside him. "Just to the left, throw yourself forward, aim for above the knees, head turned to the left, both arms around the legs and GRIP."

All the training coming back to me. There was a small cloud of dust as we hit the ground together, the ball rolled loose and I grabbed it while the felled opponent, winded, gathered himself up and walked back to his friends. As I raised my eyes to my lot, I was surprised, for they were standing frozen, immobile, staring at me. I soon realised that they had never before seen a rugby tackle. "How did you do that?" A quick demonstration and soon the field was covered by small puffs of dust as tackles were practised.

Cycles used by the boys varied widely from ladies models of the 1900's, repainted and overhauled, to quite modern machines with all accessories. Tyres were a problem. Gaiters of leather or canvas were often slipped between the tube, much patched, and the hole or crack in the tyre. These thumped abominably, but worse by far was the hosepipe tyre. This was made by wrapping a piece of hosepipe around the rim and securing it with a wire inserted down the length of the 'tyre' which was then tensioned and twisted to secure it. You cannot believe how heavy and hard these tyres were to ride, they were second best to nothing at all.

I recall riding to school one fine spring morning with a friend, Derek Kalber whose father owned a canning plant in St. Clement's Road. Derek was a mild mannered boy and his bike was almost new, bought just before the Germans arrived. Riding on the righthand in single file, both requirements of our 'masters,' we had passed the Animal Shelter, when we approached two Feldgendarmes on duty wearing their Gorgets. As Derek passed on the righthand side of one, they were walking on the road towards us, he quite deliberately thrust out his jackboot so that Derek had to bump over it and was stopped by this.

A big hand gripped his handlebar and although Derek apologised for his 'mistake' and gently attempted to extract his bicycle, the German never moved or spoke, nor did he ease his grip. They never touched my old bike. After several minutes, yes, actually several minutes of this statuesque performance, Donald was forced to leave his cycle and walk off with me, I could not offer him a ride on my crossbar, as that was 'verboten' too. Derek hoped that his father could recover his cycle, but that never happened. These two Felgendarmes had decided to steal it and had lain in wait for Derek, having noticed that he came up that road every day.

When the Occupation ended, neither Francis nor I returned to the Beeches, but in 1946 attended the Salesian College near Oxford as boarders.

So shoot!

Chapter Eleven   **THE BAVARIAN SERGEANT**

One autumn morning in 1942, Ken Richardson, our farmer friend and my father were standing talking in the farm courtyard at 'North Lynn' when they heard the sound of a heavily laden bicycle approaching. After a moment, there appeared the standard Wermacht cycle with heavy carriers back and front and all the usual elaborate and clumsy gear normally associated with these machines, a worthy product of the Teutonic military mind. On top of this and dominating it was a broadly built sergeant, jackbooted, gloved and topped off with a silver edged forage cap. Sergeants always wore gloves and carried a large holster on their belt containing either an automatic or revolver of heavy calibre.

Bouncing to a halt, he swung a heavy leg over his saddle, pushed his machine to a nearby granite wall, pulled at his uniform and walked heavily over to the waiting pair. "Gut morning ", he said, in heavily accented English and pushed out a gloved paw to Ken who took it. The sergeant then turned to my father with his hand still on offer, "Who is your friend, Mr Richardson?" he asked looking straight at my father. Ken muttered some introduction, but my father kept his hand pointedly by his side. Ken went on to explain that the sergeant came from time to time to claim the Wermacht's supply of oats and other crops, which farmers were obliged to grow for them. Still the gloved hand stood out and still my father kept his by his side. Slowly the big hand dropped and the sergeant scuffed his jackboots back a pace.

"You do not like me because I am a German?" he growled. My father agreed. "You were in the first one?" My father nodded knowing that this referred to the First World War. "You would like to shoot me?" The German did not expect a reply, but took my father's look for agreement. In a sudden movement he undid his holster over his left hip and drew out an automatic pistol. Pointing it up to the sky, with well-practised skill he operated the action to slide a bullet into the chamber and to Ken's surprise grabbed my father's hand and fairly slapped the heavy gun into his open palm. "There," he yelled, stepping back a pace and extending his arms out sideways from his body, "so shoot!"

Of course my father could not. "You see," said the sergeant slowly recovering his weapon, "you could not shoot me and I do not want to shoot you." He restored his gun to his holster and pushed out his hand again to my father who laughed and took it. The sergeant told them that he was from Bavaria and had a farm there and that he would much sooner be there than stuck in Jersey finding fodder for the horses. He completed his business with Ken and with a wave, pedalled methodically off. A big man in every way.

"Wo ist mein fahrrad!"

Chapter Twelve   THE WERMACHT LOSES A
BICYCLE

There was not much of any significance the ordinary person, caught up in the occupation of Jersey could do against the Germans. Too much action and hostages would be taken, this had occurred at the very beginning of the occupation when the Germans had first arrived. Several people were held in prison and later released. However, with not too much ingenuity some small things could be achieved. The bicycle was one area that proved quite fruitful in annoyance to the occupying power.

The Germans had commandeered many good civilian cycles and were often seen on Humber, Raleigh and Elswick machines, with all the best equipment and new tyres. The officers particularly seemed to enjoy the quality of a fine, green, high quality English cycle. Every bicycle they commandeered had B.E.F. and a number stamped deeply into the steering head of the handlebars, very visible against the surrounding chromium plate. The B.E.F. stood for Belshefrabher Englisher Fahrrad or Commandeered English Cycle. This did not stop us from helping ourselves to one or two of them. It was of twofold interest to us. Firstly it inconvenienced the enemy and secondly, we needed the tyres and other parts which were prohibitively expensive to buy or impossible to obtain.

Francis 'removed' one or two bicycles. His first effort was to relieve the Feldengarmerie, the German military police, of a French Peugeot with beautiful, fat, soft tyres which he coveted. This came from St. Helier, after watching it arrive several times at the Mayfair Hotel in St. Saviour's Road, a Soldatenheim or soldier's rest centre. It was not a good choice as the tyres were conspicuous, but it had to do. The frame and other pieces, which were too obvious, were consigned to a large cellar in the kitchen floor which my father had constructed.

The top was closed in with cargo hold hatches from "The Mazagan", a French barge used by the Germans to transport their supplies to the island. She had been wrecked on the reef just to the East of the Demi-des-Pas light and her cargo of Christmas supplies, butter, oranges and Cointreau had been washed up on the beach in front of the Hotel including some fine thick hatches. You will recall that Francis had actually paddled out to the wreck on a catamaran of the sort, which had been hired out to holidaymakers before the war and had brought back one or two items of food. I imagine those hatches are still there in the Marina today.

The next bicycle we 'needed' came from outside 'Bagnoles', a villa near the 'Gestapo' Headquarters at 'Silvertide' more or less opposite the Ommaroo Hotel. My father hopped onto this elegant Humber, because he admired the fine, large, leather saddle with big, chromium-plated springs. The whole machine was stripped down and hidden away for a time, but eventually was brought out to have all its transfers and badges removed. We had discovered a good source of new transfers and badges from an old cycle shop in St. Helier and these were sensitively applied. The original numbers, stamped into the frame under the saddle were filed off, the treated area built up with solder and 'new' numbers stamped before repainting. The B.E.F. number was chiselled out and filled with solder and painted neatly with black paint. We enjoyed the job and my father worked skilfully. As he said when he surveyed his handiwork, "There, its own mother wouldn't know it."

The saddle of this cycle had been its original attraction. My father must have found the vestigial saddles of the 1939 models a little uncomfortable. It was nearly to be his undoing. Pushing his cycle down Green Street, accompanying a friend who was walking; an officer was noticed coming briskly towards them from the direction of Havre-des-Pas. There was nothing unusual about this, German officers often walked. No sooner had this officer come up to them than his eye caught that saddle and he swung round without saying a word or attempting to stop the two pedestrians.

Oddly he began to peer beneath the saddle to examine the frame for numbers, and fished out of his breast pocket a piece of paper on which we must suppose he had written down the original number. Still he hung on, walking in a crouched position obviously looking for some identification. At last my father said to his friend, "I wonder what he wants," and quickly mounted the cycle and rode off leaving the officer standing in the road. The saddle was removed, and something a little less ornate was fitted.

Francis also attained a notable coup at the swimming pool at Havre-des-Pas. It was used by civilians and Germans alike, the bicycles often being parked on the raised walkway which led to the pool. Most cycles were locked, but this young officer who 'owned' a green Raleigh just leaned it against the railings and went into the pool building. Francis noticed this and we discussed it. At length, after a few days surveillance it was decided to appropriate it. When the German arrived as usual, Francis just walked out of the pool, picked up the machine and jumping on, rode it back to the Hotel where it was quickly hidden. We did not return to see how the officer was getting on.

I have mentioned elsewhere the Wermacht bicycle, this heavy, ugly, yet strong machine. Everything about it spoke brute reliability and strength. The front brake acted directly onto the tyre and was operated by rod linkage. The rear brake was a back-pedalling drum in the hub of the wheel. Large amber reflectors glowed from the pedals and large steel-framed carriers sprouted both fore and aft. The final embellishment was the pair of rifle clips on the frame. Hardly of much use for our purposes, but it had its attractions.

Every day a stout sergeant would slowly cycle past the Marina Hotel as though under orders from his doctor to lose weight. His speed was a little more than walking pace and he wobbled a little to the right and then to the left as he pressed on his pedals as though saying to himself, 'links und recht, links und recht'. The heavy tread of the tyres made a grating sound on the dusty road. We often saw him. The object of his journey was the La Plage Hotel where he no doubt carried out an inspection of the billet. Arrived at the hotel, he would stop his machine, swing a podgy leg over the saddle and with much puffing push it against the wall which bordered Billy's Lido. There he would spend a minute or two locking the machine with a large padlock and chain before pulling his uniform into some semblance of order and trudging into the hotel by the street entrance. He would stay about half-an-hour, return to his bicycle, unlock and stow his padlock and mount by placing his jackboot on a step on the rear wheel and trundle off the way he had come.

"Do you want to see murder done, Annie?" my father said with an excited smile to my mother. "Go up to Leo's bedroom and look out towards the La Plage". My room was on the second floor towards the street end of the building and afforded a good view of Billy's Lido, the pre-war, open air dance floor with its remains of once gay coloured lights dangling in the breeze. "Why, what are you going to do?" My mother asked. "Never you mind," was the reply, "Just you go away up and watch." My mother told us later that as she watched, the sergeant arrived as usual, locked up and went inside. A few minutes passed and my father appeared walking towards the Wermacht property. Without waiting, he just lifted the bicycle onto his shoulder and walked back to the Marina, opened up the kitchen cellar and dropped the machine down and closed the hatch. They both returned to my bedroom like naughty, excited children to await results.

They had not long to wait. Out came the sergeant fumbling for his key and stopped, facing the blank wall. He could not get it into his head that his bicycle had gone. At last he turned around and looked all around without changing his position and only after a few minutes, reacted by running, if you could call it that, into the La Plage. Out came the men in all sorts of undress. Braces, vests, undone jackets were all on display as perhaps a dozen men ran everywhere looking behind walls and many unlikely places, alas to no avail.

Meanwhile, up in Leo's bedroom my staid and proper parents were crying with laughter. When I came home from school they could hardly tell me for laughing, especially at the sight of the NCO shambling off towards the East with a very red face. We used the tyres that proved to be of French manufacture, but the rest of the machine just stayed out of sight. Today it does not seem of much consequence, but at that time this useless little act cheered us up no end. We felt that a blow had been struck against the authority of the Third Reich.

'Havre-des-Pas 1942'

Chapter Thirteen   LEAFLETS AND ORG TODT

It was an unforgettable sight. As the British aircraft flew over the island at night, our British aircraft making us feel so near to them and yet so far away, the anti-aircraft batteries let fly at them with everything they had. The deadly tracer rounds drew gentle arcs of great length so slowly through the sky. A fireworks display, but with much, much more noise. We were so well situated to enjoy the spectacle as the Marina Hotel was built right up to the very edge of the promenade at Havre-des-Pas with only its narrow width between us the sea and France some thirty miles away. We knew that the tracer shells and bullets were very dangerous for our airmen, but they never hit anything that we ever saw.

As soon as the firing started, we would all climb the stairs to a room with the best view in that direction and watch, usually for ten minutes or so until the last desultory shot had arced away. The most impressive sight was what we called 'flaming onions', a name my father had recalled from the 1914-1918 conflict. The 'onions' appeared to be a series of large shells fired in pairs in a lengthy stream. They spurted coloured light and climbed so slowly into the night sky. Sometimes we would hear a piece of shrapnel whirr past before it hit the promenade or road with a sharp metallic ring, but little damage was caused. We sometimes found the shrapnel lying about in the morning light, small pieces of sharp, ragged metal often with machining marks or figures stamped into them. They often felt quite warm.

'Window' as it was called was a mystery to us, for we knew nothing of its Radar jamming properties let alone about Radar itself. We just knew that the long silver strands that we found in tangled hanks of various sizes were from our planes and it felt good to touch because of this. Interesting though the 'window' was, the leaflets, which often accompanied it held our attention. Leaflet dropping happened quite frequently and they usually fluttered to the ground over a wide area. Francis and I used to find them as we went to school in the morning, when we quickly hid them out of sight in case the Feldgendarmerie should snatch them from us. It was against orders to carry, distribute or to read them.

Arriving at school, we would find that other boys from all over the island would have a few too and we were quick to calculate the spread of the latest edition. Sometimes boys perhaps from the West of the island would have some and the rest of us depended on their goodwill. Soon, like the phonecards of today, the leaflets became a collector's craze with swaps going on to obtain a complete set. We did not bother to read them much as most of it was above our heads and written in German, "Nachrichtten fur die Truppe" was a common banner at the head of many leaflets.

German had become a compulsory language in schools throughout the island and my class had a German army nurse to teach us. Most of us were studious not to apply ourselves to learning this hated language, but some, encouraged by small prizes, did try too hard. We used the Berlitz Direct Method. "Was ist das? Das ist ein bleischtift," would croon the nurse holding up a pencil and then we would intone, "Was ist das? Das ist ein bleischtift", in response and so on. Another ploy was to get us to sing jolly, German hunting songs such as, 'Gar lustig sind die jagerei alhier auf gruner heid.'

You may recall from your own experience that boys are very self conscious about their voices and that most would sooner die than sing in public, so you can imagine that the nurse was somewhat disappointed. So our German lessons did not help us to read our leaflets. Now had the nurse offered to translate them, that might have made us more attentive.

However, in a classroom there is always two levels of consciousness, firstly, what the pupils know and secondly, what the teacher knows and she was not aware of our packs of leaflets.

I woke up in the early hours one morning as tracer fire and bangs and thumps echoed around Havre-des-Pas. I sat up in bed and rested my elbows on the windowsill, for I had placed the head of my bed alongside my window for just such an eventuality. After I had been watching the display for several minutes, there was an almighty crash alongside my room in the little courtyard of 'Rocquaine,' the house next door. It was too dark to see and as it was a cold night, I decided to leave the investigation of this crash till it was light. I fell asleep, but was up before the family, dressed and crept downstairs then out onto the road where curfew was still in force. I opened the gate to 'Rocquaine' and immediately saw that the small, asbestos panelled garage was in ruins. It looked as though an earthquake had hit it and looking up to the hotel, I could see just how close my room was to the former garage.

Strangely the garage double doors were still intact and padlocked with a chain. But there was no problem in seeing into the interior, as the sides and back were non-existent, just small pieces of asbestos sheeting everywhere. There among the wreckage lay a large bundle of leaflets, about a foot thick and still tied round with strong tape. Little wonder there had been such a crash. Some bored RAF crew must have decided to throw it out complete without cutting the tape. Whatever happened, several pounds weight of paper had hurtled down from a few thousand feet and was not going to stop too quickly when it hit something, hence the wrecked garage. It was fortunate that it did not hit the hotel's slate roof, it would have gone through roof, ceilings and floors.

What a find for a collector. I quickly lifted my find and keeping an eye out for Germans, regained the hotel. I could hardly wait to see which edition this was. It was a new one. My family were all surprised to see the pile on the kitchen table when they came downstairs and with the exception of my mother, helped themselves so that they could distribute a few. I hid the rest, but took a bundle to school. No other boy had any, I had the market to myself and was being offered rare ones to complete my collection for just one of mine. At the end of the day or so, for I had to wait for some to come in the following day, I had a complete set of leaflets and my interest waned at once. So much for success.

We often thought that the Germans went around at first light gathering up the leaflets which were aimed at their troops and that sometimes they dropped their own leaflets from a much lower height for their men to find. One that seemed to fit the bill was a rather smutty and explicit booklet aimed, or so we thought, at showing soldiers how to fake illness.

At about this time, there was a strange incident in New Street that may have been inspired by leaflets in as much as it looked like sabotage. In a store used by the Germans, where the printers now stand today, the Germans had made use of the upper floor to service and store sidearms. A fire broke out and after it was brought under control, I watched from the shelter of Voisin's doorway as soldiers literally shovelled pistols of all sorts, many in bright leather holsters into a waiting lorry standing beneath the open, first floor, loading doors. There was the small automatic in pigskin or calf holsters, much favoured by the higher ranking officers and the large weapons issued to others such as the eternal Luger and many revolvers of the sort carried by the Organisation Todt. It was all mixed with wet ash and rubble. I never found out how this fire had started or what became of the weapons.

Mention of the Organisation Todt, or the Org Todt, for that was what they had inscribed on their left sleeve ribbon in Gothic script, still causes an intense distaste to rise up in me. I have reason to say that they were in my personal experience, cruel, gross bullies of the worst sort and little better than slavedrivers. They were supposed to be the paramilitary organisation responsible for all military engineering such as the construction of the bunker system, no doubt they executed it all tolerably well, but not without causing much human suffering.

A narrow gauge railway was built to carry materials such as sand and timber, this little railway, cheerful enough in itself, was built following the line of the old Jersey railway which had discontinued service in 1938. No track bed had existed in the Havre-des-Pas area, so without further ado, the Germans ripped up the tarmac outside the hotel and along the road to St. Clements Coast Road and installed the narrow track. This meant a lot of hard labour in the days before J.C.B.s, but the Org Todt did not mind, they had plenty of labour in the form of Russian and other prisoners.

Many times I saw these poor men, dishevelled is too generous a word to describe the state they were in, for it seems to suggest that they were recently quite tidy and only some recent event has affected their appearance. Abject dirt and hunger is a more fitting description. They had never seen proper food or sanitary conditions since their capture, wherever and whenever that may have occurred. We felt for them and would often comment on what we had seen. The brutes of the Org. Todt, well-fed, big men, kept them under close guard as they worked and were armed with big, holstered revolvers over their left hip and often carried a whip in their right hand. The whip had a short leather strap at its tip and its length would be about a metre.

We still have one, a grim reminder and on the handle near the leather loop which went over the wrist there is clearly stamped the Nazi Eagle and the date of manufacture. It may be said that these were meant for use by wagon drivers, to stir up the horses and I have no doubt that they often were, but I have seen them put to this other use. The khaki uniform of the Org. Todt. set them apart from the Wermacht with whom they seemed to have little in common, but the German soldiers seemed to be unaware of the suffering under their very noses. Maybe they knew better than to remonstrate with this gang.

On several occasions, when the work party was near our high fence, not six feet away from them, my father would open the gate slightly to watch the guard. As soon as the guard was preoccupied further away, he would signal to the two or three Russians who were nearest to come quickly inside our fence. With the gate closed, he would offer them whatever we had to spare, sometimes no more than a little bread and raw potatoes, which they devoured on the spot. Once I saw them take the small, wizened turnips that lay in a potato box near the gate and eat them earth and all without hesitation.

Yet beneath their rough exteriors beat generous hearts and some were educated men. A man among them, wearing what may have once been a city suit, for you could hardly tell, stopped the others before they turned to leave and sought out frantically where his left, jacket pocket might once have been, the remains of its pocket lining. You must strain your imagination to see this poor, kind man, dressed like something from a play, in loops of cloth hanging from his shoulders. Searching and at last finding a tiny piece of soap about the size of a small coin, which he pressed upon my father with appealing gestures of thanks and friendship. My father was a sensitive man and I could see the tears start to his eyes as he clasped the man's hands in his and forced him to keep his 'treasure'. We saw them out of the gate in the same way that they had come in. We were never caught doing this.

One young Russian, managed to come in more than once and with the help of his friends who must have covered for him, stayed for a short time and was brought into our kitchen. My mother warmed to him and found some small treat, but his eyes fastened on a woodworking plane, which was lying on the kitchen worktop. He hurried across to it and picked it up with real pleasure and began to mime using it, to show us that he was a carpenter in peacetime. You may gather that I have very little time for the Org. Todt. or their achievements.

We receive our deportation papers.

Chapter Fourteen   OUR PAPERS ARE RECEIVED

We used to obtain our 'Evening Post' and my father's tobacco ration, all 2ozs of it, from Carter's newsagent's shop in Colomberie. Although the 'Evening Post' was full of German propaganda it also contained such essential reading as the 'Exchange and Mart' column where we read such advertisements as, 'Cycle tyre size 26" x 1½" for sale or exchange for a laying hen or what?' The tobacco was not smoked, but used for just such exchanges, while my father, who did smoke, made do with cherry leaf tobacco made from dried cherry leaves or home-grown tobacco cured with molasses. He seemed to enjoy it, at least he never complained!

It was late afternoon when I called in to collect our paper, and found the small shop full with perhaps eight or ten people. Quite a crowd when you recall that the Germans did not allow gatherings of more than five. "You will be among the first to go". I did not know what Mr. Carter meant as he handed me our paper, but I saw that all eyes were on me. "I don't understand," I said. "There is an order in the paper saying that all the English residents are to be deported to Germany," I was told.

I was not in the least shocked by this news. Apart from the usual mistake in which I was referred to as English when I was born in Edinburgh the announcement filled me with some excitement. Soon we would be travelling again, my father, mother, Francis and me. I came out in reply with some silly remark addressed to everyone about how much fun it would be and how we would look forward to it, then got on my bike and pedalled furiously home to break the news.

You may well imagine that I was disappointed with the reception, which my 'news' received from my parents. I tried to convince them that it was good news, but was soon told to "Whisht," which is good Scots for "Be quiet." Looking back, I can see that my parents had enough to bother about with this news without my childish nonsense.

Not many days after this, at about midday, there was a loud knocking on the outer door of the Hotel and my father went to answer it. Through a side panel of glass we could see a policeman in uniform who was known to us and also a German Unteroffizier holding a clipboard. On the door being opened, the policeman explained that he was accompanying the German to give us our deportation orders for tomorrow and began to explain further. His take-it-or-leave-it attitude and actual presence in our States Police uniform was too much for my father.

He exploded in anger and dressed down this unworthy representative of the law. He told him, among other things, that when the war was over and we had won, he would see him prosecuted. At first taken aback, the policeman stammered out some apology and weak excuse, but when this did not abate my father's anger he became abusive. The German shoved his papers at my father and told him to have the family at the harbour at the given time and to leave our keys with the German authority, labelled for reference. It still rankles to think that we were to be ordered off the island with the assistance of the police.

According to the Order, we were to be allowed one suitcase each of clothing and personal items, the keys to the Hotel were to be left with the Germans and all details of other property was to be given to the Occupying Power. It was unbelievable. But, great though the problems created for my parents were, there was a greater problem yet. Francis had had a serious accident while playing with a small boxcart he had made. He had been coming down Mount Bingham towards the La Plage Hotel when the front axle, assembled out of an old perambulator and on which both his feet were resting, had suddenly whipped backwards. It had hit a stone on the right-hand side and trapped his ankle between the metal of the axle and the wood of the 'chassis'. When the ambulance arrived it was found that he had not only broken his ankle, but had also damaged a tendon and artery. He was still in hospital.

When we called to see him that evening during the visiting hour, we found him very distressed. Someone had told him that we had been deported and had already left the island. He took a lot of comforting and was in a great deal of pain besides, in those days before antibiotics and analgesics. This made my father determined that we were not leaving. I was greatly disappointed.

From that time my father summoned up his entire native wit and determination. Our good doctor, Doctor Gow, who had his Consulting rooms in Midvale Road was the first to receive a visit. He was persuaded that we had come down to Jersey from Scotland on medical advice, as my mother was so ill that a change to a warmer climate was essential. The good doctor took no persuading and in the best traditions of the medical service, cobbled together an armoury of documents to impress the Germans. The fact that my brother was in hospital might have delayed our departure, but not even that was certain. a positive exemption had to be obtained.

Enquiries established that attendance at the Feldkommandturiat at College House on Mont Millais was mandatory, if we hoped to be exempted. My mother and father set off on foot and were away for hours. I was torn between hope that we would go and a growing fear that all would not be well if we did go. A certain maturity was being forced upon me by events. At last they returned. The German doctor who had examined my mother was an elderly man and had been very kind and understanding. He did not feel that she should go and issued a paper to say so, with many rubber stamp marks. Francis was so pleased when he heard the news that evening that it marked a turning point in his convalescence.

However, sadly other good friends were not to be so fortunate and time and time again we said goodbye to friends. Among those who came to say goodbye was Mr. and Mrs. Wilkinson who owned the sweet shop and sweet factory that stood on the corner of Little Green Street and Colomberie. They had received their marching orders in much the same way as we had, but were allocated to a later consignment of deportees. They had four children to consider too. Peggy their eldest was a teenager, but Gordon was my age and Michael was his younger brother and there was a baby, Theresa. They brought with them some of their private store of food, which they had decided to divide among their friends and I seem to recall that we were given large tins of about 7lbs weight each of corned beef.

We spent a very long time chatting to them and discussing all the possibilities, not least among them the present state of the war. At last they prepared to leave and my father said that he would help them in the morning with their luggage, such as it was. You must remember that we were all quite undernourished and consequently weak, so that to carry luggage from Colomberie to the Albert Quay was a heavy task.

In the morning my father accompanied them to the harbour, their papers were checked and they joined a queue to go aboard.

Mrs. Wilkinson was anxious to get aboard quickly to secure a good place for the sea crossing to St. Malo. The wait was going to be a long one, so my father offered to take the older children for a walk to keep them from becoming bored. This was agreed and off they went. The 'walk' continued towards St. Aubin as my father, on the spur of the moment, saw the possibility of preventing their departure at all. When at last they returned it was to find that the boat had left, but without the Wilkinson family. The Germans were furious, but my father explained that he thought that the boat was to leave later and after much verbal abuse and threat the family was told to go and that they would be on the next boat. There never was another boat. We were pleased to be able to return the corned beef to Mr.and Mrs. Wilkinson.

I had a narrow squeak from being arrested by the Germans when the first pitiful company was to leave the harbour. It was late afternoon and I had taken my cycle up to Mount Bingham to see the departure of the first deportees. I would have been warned not to go had I said where I was going before I left home, so I just said that I was going for a 'ride'. My recollection is of a dull afternoon made more depressing by the impending departure. What could now happen to all of us left on the island? We were at the mercy of an unscrupulous enemy issuing orders, which affected our every activity. I rode to the middle of Pier Road, just to the point where the entrance to the multi-storey car park now stands. From here I had an uninterrupted view over the whole harbour.

Against the far berth on the Albert Quay where the mailboats Isle of Sark and Isle of Guernsey used to stand before the war, a squat, camouflaged ship was loading our friends and compatriots. We watched. We, because I joined a small group of similarly minded people, curious to see what would happen.

The group slowly grew, well beyond the magical German figure of five. Perhaps two hundred people stood around watching intently. Camaraderie grew amongst us too and we all chatted earnestly and anxiously. At last, with some bustle, the ship began to move imperceptibly. It was the catalyst we had not expected.

At first we just called out words of encouragement using the colloquialisms of the Tommy Hanley era, but then nostalgia settled over the crowd and a lone male voice began to sing. The words carried clearly over the water and buildings and were soon taken up by us all. With some volume we rendered, 'There Will Always be an England,' 'Land of Hope and Glory' and 'God Save the King'. As we finished our first verse, we became aware of the voices from aboard the ship faintly carrying across to us as the deportees joined in. We fell to the next verse with renewed vigour and the most amazing feeling of 'oneness' with those people came over us all.

Suddenly, to our right a detachment of steel helmeted soldiers advancing in a line across the road with rifles carried across their chests came quickly at us. People around me swirled and panicked. Who could blame them? We did not know what these troops would do. I had difficulty in disentangling my cycle from the crowd around me and had to delay my departure somewhat or risk losing it. Everything seemed to be happening in slow motion. At last I could move. As I turned my cycle towards Mount Bingham and just as I landed on its saddle, so a large, gloved hand landed on my crossbar and gripped it. The glove was knitted of field green wool and was as common a glove as you could ever wish to see, but its presence firmly wrapped around my polished crossbar is unforgettable. It meant arrest, rough treatment, shouting, detention and Heaven knows what else.

With strength from nowhere, I joined both my hands together in a sort of double fist and raising them above my head, brought them down on the back of the gloved hand. I never saw the face, the helmet, the uniform. Nothing. My hands hurt with the blow, but with a loud German expression which I took to be pretty rude, the hand was rapidly withdrawn. I stood up on the pedals and put all my strength into the effort, the back tyre spurted as it slipped on the dusty road and I was lying low now over my handlebars in case there should be a shot. I was soon through the leaders of the running crowd and away. To my right the ship was lining up to pass through the pierheads. But for my father, we would have been on that ship, but I never gave it a glance.

We never felt secure from deportation until the Allied Forces had taken St. Malo. Our fears were real, some of those who left died in the camps and although they were often treated kindly by the German population, they led deprived, communal lives lacking real privacy. Had Hitler thought it expedient he would have held their lives as of little worth against some possible gain in his evil plans.

The Leutnant's Citroën

Chapter fifteen   SOME MINOR INCIDENTS

I cannot be sure that it is true, but one incident was commonly reported at the time and it amused all who heard about it. André Citroën was a brilliant car designer and his Citroën Light Fifteen of the pre-war years was ahead of other cars in its construction and particularly in its cornering and roadholding ability. It received acclaim from one unexpected quarter, namely officers in the Wermacht. One young officer had managed to find a prime example of the marque in Jersey and had commandeered it for his own use. Duty one day called him to pay a visit to the Springfield sports ground in St Helier. On arriving at the ground, he parked his car on the end of the row of vehicles already there and went into a nearby office.

The Renault tank, equally as French as the Citroën, was a light tank, not up to the needs of the Wermacht, but they had captured a good number of them in occupied France. The gun turrets on these tanks seemed suitable for defensive employment on the bunkers being built along the Atlantic coast of Europe and if you look closely today, you will still see one or two in place in Jersey. This left the tank without a turret, but still useful as a sort of bulldozer. One or two of these turretless tanks came to Jersey and the one I am thinking about came to Springfield to do a particular job.

Good, British cars commandeered by the Germans were sent off the island for sale, I believe in neutral countries. Less saleable cars were still valuable to the German war effort for their metals. A complete car for melting down was too bulky to ship, so the idea of flattening them was accepted. The best tool in Jersey for this work was the Renault tank. Just drive it over the cars set up in a row and there you have flattened cars.

Do you recall the Citroën Light Fifteen parked neatly at the end of the row of cars? The young officer came out of the office to find his pride and joy as flat as all the other cars. Naturally he was annoyed and even more so when he remembered his personal belongings in the car, particularly his briefcase and gold cigarette case on the shelf beneath the dashboard. When he had stopped shouting, obliging German soldiers, on duty crushing cars, found themselves trying to disentangle a Citroën with crowbars and other levers. It was said that the officer eventually got his property back, but everything had been destroyed by the weight of the tank. Even if it had not been true, it made a good story and cheered us up at a bad time in the war.

Similarly, after Dunkirk, the Wermacht had acquired many British trucks and their spares. The lightweight Bedford and Austin were based on the civilian version. Some German recognised that there was a good number of the civilian lorries in Jersey of these makes and decided that they should be added to the collection. Now the little Bedfords and Austins were our farmers' most popular choice to transport their crops around the island to the Weighbridge. It hurt them greatly to have to take them to Sringfield for inspection and possible loss to the Wermacht.

Some lorries were rejected as being too old or too worn, but others were taken from their owners; all except one. My father had been much involved with military vehicles in the First World War, mainly the Ford 'T' model and he knew the requirements of the transport officer. Ken Richardson, his farmer friend had a very nice little Bedford one and a half tonner, just what the German wanted. He told my father about his problem and after some thought my father said to him, "Do you know of a good blacksmith you can trust completely?" Ken did. The lorry was driven to the blacksmith somewhere in St. Martin and my father showed him where he wanted an irregular ring of welding around the rear axle. This was done to his satisfaction. He then rusted and aged the welding and rubbed grease and road dirt into it until it looked fairly old.

Ken took the lorry into town for inspection. A sergeant in fatigues was in charge. "Nix gut," said Ken pointing to his lorry. The sergeant came over to take a closer look and Ken ducked down low at the back, pointing to the welding and saying as trained, "Nix gut". The sergeant knew a broken and badly repaired axle when he saw one and he also knew that the truck could not carry its full payload. It could break down at any time and would be a nuisance. "Caput, caput," he yelled at Ken having noticed Ken's ability to speak German. "Raus," he yelled shoving the rejection paper into Ken's lorry. A delighted Ken left at once, with his lorry.

On his way back to the Marina hotel one afternoon, Francis noticed the men barrowing very large sacks of flour, each containing one hundred kilograms, towards the lorries on the road. There had been a minor fire in the Old Blue Coach garage down a short driveway opposite the Carlton Hotel and it had been decided to move a large consignment of flour, all contained in sacks, on which was emblazoned a large Wermacht eagle. The labour force was all civilian, mostly Spaniards and quite young. Francis thought he would join them for a bit of do-it-yourself flour collecting.

We had a small sack barrow at home, not unlike the ones being used by the men. Francis wheeled this down to the garage and picked up his sack like all the other men. The tug up the slope to the road was hard going, but he reached the top and instead of joining the queue to load a lorry he continued to his right and was soon back at the hotel quite unnoticed by the busy work detail down the road. The flour was quickly transferred to other containers and the sack hidden away. We looked at it more than once after the Occupation had ended, but we enjoyed the flour for many months before that.

Fred Langlois the auctioneer prospered during the occupation due to his hard work and the needs of the Jersey people to buy and sell to sustain life. I often attended the auctions held in a small store near the Wesley Chapel in Grove Street. Jersey had been an attractive place for expatriates coming home from abroad before the war. It had a very low cost of living, a good climate and was close to the United Kingdom. Some died in Jersey during the war and their effects were sold at auction. Some of the items had not been unpacked for many years and were very interesting. Complete suits of fine Japanese armour were not uncommon, they even had the lists of the armourers who made each part and fitted into the original boxes. Many items like this passed under Fred's hammer for a shilling or two. They would be worth a lot more today.

Having prospered, the firm bought the premises they occupy today in Don Street and Fred set up his office there. My father knew Fred Langlois quite well through business and was in his office when a clerk burst in to say that there was a group of Germans heading for the office at that moment to search it. Mr. Langlois jumped to his feet and threw open a cupboard from which he pulled out a 16mm cine camera, a Paillard Bolex that the Germans strictly forbade islanders to possess. He was beside himself with anxiety and could not think how to get rid of it. My father took it out of his hands and pushed it under his own overcoat and holding it with one hand just walked out of the office and across the shop floor as the Germans approached the office door. No one stopped him. He returned the camera to

Fred Langlois the following day.

Francis played a prank, which might have had serious consequences, early on in the history of the narrow gauge German railway. He had heard or perhaps seen on film how trains were derailed by explosives, usually dynamite, in the standard Western and decided to have a go himself. Sodium chlorate based explosives are notoriously unstable and should never be made up, but Francis knew some of the risks and having made a batch filled a narrow sausage made of cloth with it. This he inserted unseen into the points at the bottom of Mount Bingham near the Green Street junction. He kept well away and waited. At last a diesel locomotive chugged along pulling a line of steel trucks, such as you would find in a mine. On passing over the explosives, there was a loud bang and the train came to a halt. The driver came down and inspected his wheels and the track, but found nothing amiss and carried on, much to the disappointment of our saboteur.

Worse was to follow. The Germans had captured two American airmen and my father, Francis and me were standing on the pavement outside the hotel, when we saw an armed guard of about twelve men escorting one of the airmen from the direction of the Swimming Pool towards Mount Bingham. Without thought, my father dashed inside and came out with his tobacco ration, a silver foil covered block weighing about two ounces, and quickly put it into Francis' hand saying something to the effect of slipping it to the American. Francis walked alongside the soldiers looking for an opportunity, but the street was empty and there was no diversion he could use. So, suddenly, rather than let my father down, he ran between the soldiers and attempted to give the block to the airman who held his hands up in the air and said, "No son". This left Francis with nothing to do but run, which he did towards the hotel now some fifty yards off.

My father's action had been ill-considered and out of character, but he now thought swiftly and said loudly enough for Francis to hear as he neared us, "Not to the hotel. Go down Farsley." This was the lane opposite to the hotel. He was obviously afraid that if Francis ran into the hotel the Germans would follow and arrest him. By now the German corporal in charge had unslung his rifle and was chasing after Francis shouting "Halt." Francis ran as fast as he could go and turned away from us.

The corporal operated his bolt as his jackboots slid to a stop at the top of the lane and he took aim. My heart almost stopped as the whole picture froze in my mind of Francis running and the guard levelling his rifle. Suddenly the guard lowered his Mauser and swearing to himself made his way back to his men. They marched off and, a good while later, Francis came back with the tobacco. My father was very shame-faced about his well-intentioned action that almost cost Francis his life. I think the American was Lieut. Haas. Francis 'bumped' into him in later in prison.

Renault tanks in 1945

Renault tank gun turret, Green Street, Havre-des-pas

The turrets were everywhere

'The Rover is prepared'.

Chapter Sixteen   CHRISTMAS EVE 1943

Cars have always figured large in my family. My father had an undying love for them and understood their temperament to perfection. On returning to Edinburgh in 1919 he had established a prosperous bus and coach business and garage from which he had become quite wealthy. Now, in the dark days of 1943, the Germans had been confiscating cars, to scrap them for their steel or to sell them to neutral Sweden for hard currency. The form was that the owner of a vehicle was identified from Motor Taxation records and a German N.C.O. would visit the owner and inspect the car. If it proved to be at all acceptable a worthless receipt was issued and the car was towed away or driven off.

My father saw a golden opportunity to spoil a little of the Germans' game and to turn a neat profit out of it, if all went well. It was quite a risk. Through enquiries among acquaintances, he came across several cars, about twenty or more, which he bought from their owners and towed them away to hide elsewhere. I remember that he had one small store near Tunnel Street, just off the Esplanade in which he hid five or six good cars. I can see them now and recall the odour of stale petrol and drying oils, as they stood trapped in a time warp of a war and yet eloquent of many pre-war spins in the countryside and much happier times.

I used to enjoy climbing in behind their steering wheels and gazing over their long bonnets past their characterful radiator caps all the while imagining, as only a young boy can imagine, the long roads and hills stretching out before me. There was a Citroën 12 of 1938 that I particularly liked. It was pale grey and had very attractive wheels spooked like fans in a turbine. Nearby stood a Wolseley Hornet convertible with a delightful

Tickford, two door body and a hood which wound up and down by turning a large handle which fitted a hole near the back and there were others. I would leave this store and step out into the street among the Germans and the drab cheerless life of the occupied island carrying a dark, but enjoyable secret, feeling a little uplifted and waiting for the war to end.

But other cars were hidden elsewhere in ones and twos. My father always liked Rovers and had acquired a black Rover 14 of 1934 from a Mr. Le Brun who was, I believe, a baker in St. Martin. This car was towed behind a horse during the lunchtime, when most Germans were enjoying their siesta, to the Marina Hotel. Once inside, behind our own high fence, we camouflaged it under a pile of wooden flooring from the old chapel we had dismantled. It was quite invisible. However, in late 1943 the Germans began looking for fuel and it was felt that if they came in to search our hotel, the timber pile would have yielded one surprise too many. My father looked around for another hiding place.

Ken Richardson of North Lynn Farm in Trinity had become a good friend and my father often spent the day with him sometimes helping with repairs and other things. Ken had asked my father to find a car for him and a large 1938 Vauxhall Sixteen had been bought and hidden in his barn under a load of straw. There was just room for another car alongside the Vauxhall and Ken agreed that the Rover should go there. There was a problem as it was a long haul for a horse from Havre-des-Pas to Trinity and all uphill for six miles.

The simple solution was to drive the car there. Now only very few cars were given permits for use by doctors and some essentially employed civilians. German vehicles were quite scarce too, as fuel was in short supply. The Germans often used horsedrawn carts and peculiar grey military wagons and even used the rear portion of cars fitted with shafts for the horse. Bicycles were everywhere.

Ken, with true Jersey hospitality, had invited us to join his family for Christmas and to stay on a few days after. This was wonderful news, because Mr. and Mrs. Richardson were very generous and prepared lavish meals at Christmastime.

Our family was near starvation point; living on meagre rations supplemented with an extra pint of milk or portion of butter brought back from 'North Lynn'. My father struck upon the idea of driving his Rover to 'North Lynn' on Christmas Eve when it was dark. Gradually he obtained the two or three gallons of petrol required, some of it siphoned from his other cars. At last he had enough. Much time was spent the day before, uncovering the car, fitting a battery and making preparations. One major problem appeared, which was to have a considerable effect on our journey.

The car was not fitted with blackouts on its headlights as it had been laid up for the duration of the war. The blackouts were mandatory in every country at war and were essential for any vehicle on the roads in those days. The sidelights were blackened with shoe polish, as was the tail light. The right-hand headlamp had its bulb removed completely, but the remaining powerful headlight would not respond to shoe polish and so a black cloth was found and placed over the headlamp which was the typical, egg shaped, chromeplated unit of the 1930's car. The cloth was firmly secured with string. We were ready.

Excited by our impending adventure we could not wait for the hour to come when, after four long years, we would find ourselves once again on the open road. Just after curfew at nine o'clock, for we lived within the curfew zone demarcated by a broad red band painted along the pavement, the gate was cracked open and a watch kept for the two man German patrol coming as usual from the east and moving towards Mount Bingham. At last they shuffled past with felt pads strapped over the steel shod soles of their jackboots. Steel helmets glistened in the moonlight, which also picked out the muzzles of the rifles slung over the shoulders of their greatcoats. When they were out of sight, we swung open the double gates on well-oiled hinges and silently pushed our Rover out on to the frosted road.

The gate was closed and my mother took her favourite rear seat on the left-hand side of the car. Francis slipped into the front seat alongside my father while I quietly closed my door at the back. My mother's gloved hand squeezed mine tightly and we all laughed quietly with nervous anticipation as my father switched on the ignition and depressed the tiny starter button that Rover then used on the Startix system. The engine purred on all six cylinders. We glided forward towards the east, passing the Swimming Pool, the Ommaroo Hotel and turned up St Clement's Road. The single headlight gave a little too much light, but we were not prepared to stop to make adjustments. Passing Howard Davis Park, we were soon driving in style at forty miles per hour up Mont Millais.

The chance of meeting a solitary German soldier had been weighed and discounted, but we knew that the German Headquarters at College House could be a problem to be negotiated with care. The Feldkommandturiat usually bustled with activity, but we doubted that much would be happening on Christmas Eve. As we rounded the long bend, driving as required on the right-hand side of the road, we suddenly saw trouble.There they were, a seven-man patrol in single file with a corporal leading them, a Schmeisser 9MM machine pistol across his chest. The patrol was marching down the left-hand pavement towards us and had a clear view of the Rover as we approached. The corporal's steel helmet tilted a little as he looked in our direction. Our hearts beat faster. The Rover kept on.

Then just at this most crucial moment, disaster struck. The black cloth that had obscured our left-hand headlamp, the headlamp which was lit and which had no other blackout, slipped back and lay fluttering in the breeze alongside it. The light flared out into the night like a searchlight. In the total darkness of the blackout its effect was magical. Even before my father could react, the corporal barked out an order and the file halted and left turned to face the road. Rhythmic movements produced a line of rifles held perfectly at the salute and the corporal flung up his arm in the Nazi salute. We sailed past. As soon as we were out of sight all the lights were put out and the speed increased sharply along the moonlit road.

Why had this happened? We could only imagine that the patrol could not believe that this was other than an officer returning to the Feldkommanturiat. The arrogant 'flash' of light had confirmed this and wasn't that the usual unit flag fluttering on its short staff on the left mudwing? Salute it.

After a pleasant drive with no further adventures, we arrived at 'North Lynn' and we were met by the Richardsons in jubilant mood. Our arrival by car had been a well-kept surprise for them. It was a small victory, but how we enjoyed it and laughed as the story was retold.

You're no coming in here wi' yon dirty gun!

Chapter Seventeen   AN UNLIKELY ANGEL

Sister Morgan was a powerfully built, Scottish matron whose very appearance brooked no argument. Her voice carried far and clear in a high pitch and showed every trace of her native origins. Robed, for there is no other word for it, in her uniform with starched apron, sister's belt, medals and fob watch topped off by sister's cap, she was a formidable figure. Yet beneath all this presence, we were to discover that she was the most selfless and kind person you could wish to meet.

Francis had damaged his right eye very badly in early 1944. Like all accidents it had happened in a most unlikely way and so quickly. A German bomber, badly shot up after some mission, had crash-landed in a field in St. John during the night. A good friend, Maurice Gautier, was apprenticed to the farmer who owned the land on which the aircraft had come down so that Maurice found that he had good access to the site of the crash. A little older than me, Maurice was the older brother of my best friend Frank and he knew that I liked military 'junk', which turned up.

Searching around the field after the wreckage had been removed, he came across a small tubular object, about the size of a big cigar and heavily made in good steel. "I thought you might like this, I don't know what it is, but you can have it if it's any good to you," he said when I saw him at his home in Dicq Road one evening. I was pleased to have the object as it had come from the German aircraft and I soon realised that it was an apparently harmless bolt out of the action of one of the aircraft's machineguns. It must have been wrenched from its breech by the violence of the crash, but was itself unmarked. I wish to this day that I had never seen it.

One sunny afternoon, when I was elsewhere in the hotel, Francis decided to investigate this bolt. It was a natural thing to do for an inquisitive boy with an interest in mechanical things. Obviously the first thing to do was to dismantle it and see how it worked. Lacking only an armourer's tool kit, Francis took the bolt outside to our old vice, fastened to a wooden bench which stood in the open space where the old chapel had been. It could not have taken long to unscrew the front part of the metal tube, which fitted into the main body on a fine internal thread. Francis expected a very long, coil spring to push out the steel firing pin. Nothing moved. He took the bolt out of the vice and looked down inside the open tube to see what was holding it and at that terrible moment, the pin became unlocked and driven, by the coiled up spring and unrestrained by its cap, it flew with force into his eye. It could have killed him.

It was a terrible moment for my father as Francis came stumbling through the door into the large kitchen, incoherent with pain and shock and with his hands covering his eye. I can see my father now holding him close to him and gently using his tongue to move some of the membrane from the damaged eye back into place. The hospital was a long walk away and I waited in agony with my mother for their return. Francis was kept in hospital and Mr. Harthan, the eye surgeon, worked wonders to save his eye, but the image formed would always be distorted by the scarred tissue. Francis began his many journeys back and forward to the hospital outpatient department when he was discharged from the ward a few days later. The outpatient Department was in the Casualty area and so it was to the Casualty Department that Francis went for changes of dressing every day and so began our friendship with Sister Morgan, the Casualty Sister.

It was while still bandaged around his head and recovering from his injury, that Francis was imprisoned by the 'Gestapo' for helping himself to a German rifle. The German always prided himself on his efficiency and there was some basic humanity too, for Francis was permitted to go under armed guard each day at about noon, the short walk from the prison to the hospital which adjoined it. Sister Morgan's department was approached up the granite steps of the main entrance and turning right in the foyer, you passed through a high ceilinged waiting room to the great arched doorway of the Casualty Department. The Department gleamed. The copper and brass steriliser gleamed most of all, paying tribute to the many nurses who had polished it, as it steamed gently in the corner near a window. White curtains stood stiffly to attention reflecting in the polished floor and the smell of strong antiseptics pervaded every inch of that large Victorian room.

Sister Morgan echoed her surroundings in the cleanliness and correctness of her uniform. Heinrich and Otto were two venerable German soldiers, not frontline troops you understand, but recruited into the Wermacht as the war lumbered on and their age group was at last called up. Heinrich was tall and thin while Otto was short and quite fat, I do not doubt that both saw service in 1916. Grandfathers in uniform, it was their duty to take turns on a rota to accompany Francis to the hospital Casualty Department.

"You're no coming in here wi' yon dirty gun," Sister Morgan's tones conveyed her shock and disgust that anyone could think of such a breach of her unwritten code. "Ye can sit yersel' oot here, he'll no' be rinnin' awa'," she continued indicating with a magisterial sweep of her arm the hard wooden pew in the waiting room near the door of her sanctum. The German soldier was trained to recognise authority when confronted with it and responded without argument. And so it was that day after day, for many weeks, long after the need for any change of dressings or treatment was needed, Francis was taken to Casualty on the sole 'say so' of dear Sister Morgan.

Meanwhile, in the Casualty room itself, Sister would open an inner door leading to the corridor to the wards and draw us in. It was in this way that my mother and I and eventually my father, enjoyed an hour or so with my brother every day. At first we brought a little food with us, whatever we could scrape together and watched Francis devour it after his prison regime of thin soup and grey bread. However, this was not good enough for our 'Angel'. Hot meals began to appear from the steriliser and after she had 'trained' Heinrich and Otto, she even produced a small repast for them. I am sure that she did this from real human concern rather than for any hope of advantage over them.

"Now listen to me, Francis," she said one day when the BBC news told us that the Germans were losing the war in Europe and we had begun to fear what they might get up to in revenge. "Now listen to me, if you hear or think that anything may happen to you next door," she said, waving an arm in the general direction of the prison, "or you feel you are in any danger, you're to go oot yon door wi' your family. I'll keep yon guard here until you're well awa before I raise the alarm. Dae ye ken what I'm saying?" Francis never had to take advantage of this selfless offer, but how grateful to her we all were.

Sister was married to a charming man who was as gentle as she was strong. We learned from her that he suffered from diabetes and needed Insulin to keep well and indeed alive. As the war progressed and even the kindest of the German doctors could not obtain Insulin from France or any other country, despite all

Sisters' pleas to both civil and military authorities, the supply of Insulin failed completely. She offered, even demanded to go to France herself, asked the Germans to radio the Allies in nearby Normandy to airdrop Insulin - anything, but all her tremendous efforts were in vain. She who had helped so many, had to watch her husband slowly fade and die. Her sadness never led to bitterness and she never lost control, but showed her endless love for us all. She was a saint.

We saw her often after the Liberation and in 1948, we had the pleasure of meeting her sister who lived in Scotland and entertained them both. There could not have been a greater contrast between two people. Her sister was a small, quiet and sensitive person who moved delicately through life, but showed the same love that hid in Sister Morgan's burly frame.

D-Day
"Allied forces under the command of general Eisenhower
have landed in France"

Chapter Eighteen   INVASION

The first few months of 1944 were normal, if one can call 'normal' living under the watchful eye of an occupying and evil power. Individual members of the German forces had shown themselves human and although we did not trust them, we did not fear them either. We had been living alongside them now for four years and knew their ways, but the whole Nazi machine was evil. It was still possible that they would recommence their deportations to Germany as hostages or to protect their factories from bombing. Nevertheless in 1944 we felt normal; normally hungry, normally deprived of our freedom, normally watchful and aware. Little escapades such as our drive in the Rover to Trinity were highlights in our lives.

Food was ghastly. Grey bread and not too much of that, the cream skimmed off the boiled milk to spread on the bread and sugar beet syrup instead of jam. The syrup was quite good and was made by grating sugar beet into a pulp and boiling it. The pulp was strained off and the liquid boiled down to delicious syrup. A lengthy process, but one of our best sources of food. This reminds me of a little adventure that Francis and I enjoyed. The Germans had left Green Street barracks for some other duties elsewhere and the barracks stood locked up and deserted against their return. On the way through the barrack square to our allotment at the back, Francis and I noticed the empty buildings and lack of guards and on the spur of the moment decided to investigate the interior.

We were soon inside by forcing a sash window at the back of the building away from the road. We were tense, ready to make our exit if any movement or voices should be heard. All was quiet. Looking in each large room we noticed portions of loaves of the Wermacht rye bread, which does not go stale and was always impressed with the year of baking on top. It had a rather bitter taste, but was otherwise good. A small sack made of woven paper string was found and all the bread was collected. There was not much else of interest, just a few copies of 'Die Signal' lying about, which we also acquired. Before leaving, a thought occurred to us and we removed all the caps from the electric light switches and exposed the bare live wires. We hoped that the troops would return in the dark, in any event, they would have to replace all the switches and that would keep someone occupied for a while.

My mother was delighted with the bread, she always was when we brought home some small item of food, it must have been terribly hard for her to try to feed us all. She could be very imaginative when cooking and rose to the occasion with a giant, plum pudding, about the size and shape of a football. We were so hungry that it looked three times this size to us. Of course, she had no plums, so she used dried carrots and for sweetening she used sugar beet syrup and saccharin, the whole flavoured with nutmeg and other spices. It was hot, delicious and very filling. We ate it hot, cold, fried and as a cake until after several days it was all gone. We often spoke about it in later years.

As the 'normal' months of 1944 dragged on, we sat in the kitchen in the evening, listening occasionally to the BBC broadcasts to occupied Europe. Thanks to this we knew exactly what was happening in North Africa and in Italy. We also enjoyed drama and the 'Workers Playtime' broadcasts from a factory "somewhere in England". What a great help this was to us. Had we depended on the German news in the 'Evening Post' we might well have thought we were still occupied today. The German news was totally untrue and grossly exaggerated in their favour. It was laughable. Apart from listening to the BBC, we made up small lights out of glass screw top jars with wicks inserted through a hole pierced in the lid. These burned diesel oil, did not give out much light and smoked prettily.

However, with my young eyes I could read and so I used to read to the family for an hour or so. Jules Verne's 'The Terribore' is one book I well remember.

The weather began to get warmer, the evenings lighter. Suddenly, one June morning, my father woke up Francis and me and told us to look carefully out of the window. The normally deserted roads were a hive of German activity. Camouflage netting was stripped from the Renault tank gun turret at the head of Green Street slipway, barbed wire was strung across the street, soldiers humped sandbags into place on top of walls and 'Spandau' machineguns appeared. "Come and listen to the radio" my father said. We crept down the stairs to the kitchen and stood by the cupboard in which the radio was hidden. The little Bush was tuned by its green magic eye and turned down to a whisper. Eventually we heard the announcer, who sounded quite excited say, "The following communiqué has been issued from Allied Supreme Headquarters.... This morning Allied Forces under the command of General Eisenhower landed in occupied France".

We experienced the strongest emotions, laughing and hugging each other, we now knew why the Germans were in a tizzy. To go outside was considered too dangerous and there was no system of any sort to advise us what to do. No loudspeaker cars or prepared signals, nothing. We knew that we would be in a dangerous position when the Allies landed, but we had a deep cellar and would use that. It seemed that the Occupation might soon be over. We were very much mistaken.

At last, throughout the day the position became clearer, the

Allies were fighting for their lives to establish a foothold and only gradually did we realise that the foothold was in Normandy just thirteen miles away from the North of the island. We saw distant aircraft and heard the anti-aircraft guns had fired accidentally on a German fighter. The following days were rather restricted as we did not feel that we should draw too much attention to ourselves, living as we did inside the military zone, the red demarcation line of which passed along the edge of the pavement outside the hotel. I have no doubt, that had serious fighting started on the beaches below us, the hotel would have been used as a vantage point for a machinegun or for rifle fire. It was strange that the Germans never took over the building, although they must have considered it.

Gradually as the days wore on, we plotted the fighting in a school atlas and saw that the Allies had a firm hold on Normandy. Familiar names such as St. Lo and Avranches came up and then the Allies were away towards the South and East. By this time the Germans had stood down, but there was now a different mood about them. They could see that they were cut off and waited anxiously for the Allied Force to turn on them. Jersey had once been a prime posting for soldiers, so much better than the Eastern Front, which they dreaded, but now what would happen? For us the excitement continued for we knew at last that one-day we would be free when the Germans had been driven out of France. However, the Germans never offered to surrender, not even when it was obvious that they were completely cut off from their units in Europe by hundreds of miles of Allied territory.

A stiffening factor for the Germans was the vigorous defence put up by their troops in Normandy and later in Brittany, when the islands off St. Malo refused to surrender to the Americans and were reduced, like St. Malo itself, to ruins. Also, a Marine unit had escaped after attempting to attack the D-Day invasion fleet's Western flank and some elements of it had got to Jersey and their commanders appeared to be rabid Nazis who, we understood, refused to countenance any notion of surrendering. We were happy, the news was good and if we kept our heads down all would be well. But this was to prove more difficult than we realised and we were to move into our worst phase of the Occupation.

'Woef'

Chapter Nineteen **KARL, WOLF, ERIC, WILLY AND BERNARD**

Francis is my brother, older than I am by almost three years. He was sixteen, adventurous and embued, as indeed we all were, by the BBC transmissions into occupied Europe, to do anything he could to inconvenience the German Forces. Nicknamed 'Jock' by his close friends he had an attractive personality and was a natural leader, always willing to cook up some scheme to provide excitement and a challenge. The scheme in hand was about to provide more excitement than he or any of his friends had envisaged.

It was 1944; we had gone through the surprise and joy of the Allied invasion of nearby Normandy only a few miles distant. We had also gone through the disappointment of not being liberated immediately as we had so fondly hoped. With hindsight I can now see that any attempt to liberate the Channel Islands in 1944 would have caused a tremendous loss of life. Although we, the Islanders, had to endure another year before the Liberation in 1945, it was a wise decision and left a large contingent of German troops isolated and nearly neutralised while we were spared the pain of such towns as Caen and Avranches.

There can be no doubt that our home, the Marina Hotel, would have been right in the firing line. The Germans had settled down after their panic days of the invasion when every arrangement for repelling the expected attack had been put into place all around us. Barbed wire across the streets, machine guns in place and manned and evidence everywhere of total preparedness.

Francis had made an interesting discovery in the little road behind the Merton Hotel, on Belvedere Hill. Of course, the Wermacht occupied this modern hotel which had been the holiday destination of many young couples in pre-war days. The discovery started with a cracked pane of glass in a small frame, which gave light to a small storeroom at the back of the hotel. Leaning his cycle against the wall while sitting on it, Francis managed to remove a part of the reeded glass pane and peering through the opening, found to his pleasant surprise, a good quantity of Mauser rifles in racks. He replaced the broken glass and left the scene.

Donald Bell and Richard 'Dicky' Williams were his close friends, although a little older than him and all three had reached the age when they longed to be part of the fight against the Nazis. Informal discussions had frequently occurred which centred on how to disrupt the Germans' life in Jersey and here was the opportunity to begin to put some of this thought into practice. On hearing about the rifles, Donald and Dicky began to plan how best to secure three of these rifles so conveniently left for their collection. It was agreed that to divert suspicion from the civilian population they would leave some clues to suggest an Org. Todt involvement, for there was not much love lost between the Wermacht and this miserable organisation of slavedrivers. An Org. Todt forage cap was already in their possession and this together with another item was to be left behind for discovery by the Feldgendarmerie, or military police. Francis idled away his time in Belvedere Hill, all the time watching for any approaching trouble, while Donald and Dicky removed the pane of glass and opened the window.

Richard, with great courage, fitted his large frame into the opening and lowered himself to the floor inside the store. No one had seen them. He quickly selected three Mausers and passed them out to Donald who placed them in a sack. The 'clues' were left and the glass replaced and they had not been seen. The heavy sack, for three army rifles are very heavy indeed, was tied to a bicycle and the three walked off to Richard's home which was nearby in Don Road and there the spoils were divided up. Francis took the rifle off to the Marina and hid it well and Donald set off for his home in St Brelade where the Silver Springs Hotel stands today.

All was not to go smoothly. Cycling home, Donald was involved in a serious accident, his cycle was badly damaged and he was treated for his injuries in hospital, but the Gods smiled on our three conspirators and the rifle was not discovered. Francis and Richard spent some anxious hours after they heard about the accident wondering about Donald and about his rifle. All was well, Donald soon recovered and nothing untoward had been heard about the disappearance of rifles from the Mermaid Hotel.

Francis told his father about the rifle and found that his action was respected, after all he was nearly seventeen and many younger boys were actively resisting the Germans throughout Europe. The rifle was well hidden together with some ammunition and alongside a British Army S.M.L.E. rifle which my father had acquired for his own use. All would have been well had not another boy, who had come to know about one of the other rifles, been taken by the Germans for other offences. One cannot apportion blame for some of the events that happened during the war and the Germans could question with masterly skill interweaving threats with kindness and downright violence. Whatever happened, my father noticed unusual activity on the road near the Marina, where down a cul-de-sac, he saw Gestapo, Feldgendarmerie and civilian prisoners beside three cars.

He hurried back to the hotel and drew Francis out into the courtyard where he showed him the Germans now casually walking in their direction, but still some way off. Francis recognised the young prisoners and said so. "Take the rifles and ammunition quickly" he was told, "and go out the back way. Here's the key to Haimance Cottage. Hide them there". The cottage was used by my father as a store and stood among others, just off Ann Street. Francis quickly recovered the guns and tied and covered them on his cycle and made off. He found that he could not pedal the cycle up Green Street, because of the weight and only really managed to get going once he reached Snow Hill bus station, but eventually he reached the cottage and hid the rifles and, locking up, also hid the key.

On returning to Havre-des-Pas his worst fears were realised. Mrs. Gray, who lived in 'The Nest', a house on Mount Bingham, since demolished, called out "Francis", to stop him as he passed her in the road. Francis stopped and she hurried over to him. "Don't go back to the hotel," she said, "The Germans are there, the Gestapo and they have arrested your father." Francis was stunned; this was confirmation of his worst nightmare scenario. He realised at once that he could not leave his parents to face up to the Germans alone, so with a quick word of thanks to Mrs. Gray he headed for the hotel.

We always referred to the civilian clothed Geheim Feldpolizei as the 'Gestapo' and never thought of them as anything else, but I believe that they had some other view of themselves. It really does not matter to me, for they behaved exactly like the Gestapo and my detestation for them still lingers on after all these years and not without some cause as you may see. The 'Gestapo' had their Headquarters at No 2 Silvertide, one of two terraced houses not far from the Marina Hotel. How innocent and yet singularly sinister that this evil organisation should choose a seaside villa for their business. It could not have looked more ordinary and 'English'. Yet behind the cream painted exterior and attractive windows of this Victorian villa dwelt the members of the 'Gestapo' allocated to Jersey.

Our 'Gestapo' men favoured civilian clothes, I never saw one in the typical black uniform for which they became known. They wore suits and sported waistcoats and trilby hats. At their belt, beneath their jacket, they carried their identification medal which they showed when they announced themselves, by moving back the righthand side of their jacket with the outside edge of their right hand at the same time gripping the medal with their fingers and canting it briefly upwards.

As a boy of thirteen I was to find this all very sinister. Yet stranger still were the men themselves.
Some had been 'trained' in Canada before the war where they had learned our ways and improved their English and colloquial expressions. Oddest of all they never used their surnames. I was soon to learn never to forget the names Karl, Wolf, Eric, Willy and Bernard.

I came home from school at midday as usual, riding my bicycle; a boy's Coventry of which I was very proud and hopping off, pushed open the high wooden gate and walked straight into the 'Gestapo'. A large uniformed Feldgendarme complete with metal Gorget, seized me, my bicycle falling to the ground. I was dragged more roughly than I have ever been treated before into the hotel entrance and through into the large kitchen where the family lived during the war to gain some warmth from the friendly Aga cooker.

What warmth and comfort I normally felt in that room was

swept away as I saw both my mother and father and three or four of the 'Gestapo' in an evil mood. There was so much to take in, my stomach seized and I felt annihilated. My identity card was demanded and snatched away. I remember my father's cool and warm Scottish tones as he said, "It's all right Lovey," a term of endearment he would use when one of his family was badly hurt or shocked, "It's all right Lovey, they just want to ask a few questions." My mother was smiling and nodding encouragement to me, but I could see her whitened face and know she must have been in deep shock.

Francis was not there. He had already been taken to the prison in Gloucester Street. The 'Gestapo' seemed to know all about Francis and his friends, by this time they had seized them all. However, Francis had hidden his rifle and denied having had one. The search began. The hotel had thirty or so bedrooms, but only three in use, there were reception areas, a lounge, a restaurant, kitchen and storerooms, a large area to search. I was pushed away from my parents, who remained in the kitchen and found myself in the first floor reception area with Bernard, a junior member of Himmler's gang. I stood rooted to the floor with my heart pounding and my senses at their highest while Bernard thoroughly tore into our private home and lives.

I believe the feelings I experienced then are not unlike those of the victims of a burglary when they attempt to restore their home after the event. At last Bernard threw open an understairs cupboard and pulling out its contents found a simple, dark, grey-green cloth package about the size of a hand. Across one side was a Wermacht eagle and printing in German. Tapes fell away from the four corners and it was stuffed with medical, absorbent cottonwool.

One glance told Bernard that he had found something that was important and could lead onto other things for the package was an army field dressing. He did not know that it had come from the German bunker at the end of South Pier in St. Helier harbour, just beneath the present day St. Helier Yacht Club, nor did he know how it got into our cupboard. He knew that all he had to do was to call out "Karl", and I would have been persuaded to explain.

Francis had recruited me for the 'operation' against the bunker on South pier almost a year before. The whole pier area was a military zone and no unauthorised person was allowed into it. The area of South pier was under the same restriction, but you could pass close to the barbed wire entrance from the road that formed the edge of the old English and French harbours. The German narrow gauge railway, built to carry supplies and building materials passed over a crude bridge spanning both old harbours and from this point it could be seen that a bunker had been built under the Yacht club at the end of the pier. Bunkers meant food, iron rations and cigarettes and this one looked so inviting. Of course there would be a guard, but Francis reckoned that he and one or two friends could evade the guard if a watch could be kept on him.

This had been my job. High up on the road overlooking the pier I leaned innocently on the wall and whistled alternate signals to Francis. I can still remember one, this was the 'danger' signal when they would lie low. The 'operation' had been exciting and successful and of our share we had brought home tinned food, which we needed and some tinned cigarettes. These cigarettes were not round in section, but oval. It goes without saying, though we thought nothing of it, that to raid a German bunker in this way would have carried a severe penalty if we had been caught. But here was the good old BBC and the Morse code

'V'. Present day videos may be as stimulating to the youth of today, but I doubt it. My father did not actually encourage us to do anything, but he was proud that we did small things against the Occupying Force.

Along with our meagre supplies came the field dressing. Why we brought it, I do not know. It was a useless item meant to staunch the flow of blood from a wound. I can only imagine that in the dark we thought that it contained something useful. Bernard looked hard at the dressing in his right hand then he turned to me. "Get rid of it quick," he said softly as he pushed it into my hand and closed my fingers round it. "Quick." I flew up the stairs leading to the bedrooms and to the balconies overlooking the sea. The door to the balcony opened easily. No Gestapo had reached this level yet. I ran to the front overlooking the sea, which is engraved clearly in my mind even as I write this more than fifty years later. It was calm, almost touching the seawall, with small wavelets just caressing the beautiful sand. It was a violent contrast in its peacefulness from what was going on around me in my home at that moment. I threw the dressing out in an arc and saw it land just in the edge of the rising tide.

Suddenly I recalled the .410 shotgun that Bob Cornish, a friend of the family had found in a farm he had recently bought in St Saviour. I had admired the little sporting gun, rusty though it was, and Bob, as generous as ever, had given it to me. It was in my bedroom at the back of the hotel on this the second floor. At times like this one finds energy and decision making powers which are lacking at more casual times. I flew down the corridor, seized the gun and in a moment was hurling it out to sea. It landed further out with a splash. To throw it, I had gripped it by the barrel and as it left my hand, the bead that was the foresight on the end of the barrel, ripped the end of my forefinger. I knew that this would be difficult to explain to the 'visitors', so I pinched my forefinger tightly between the thumb and the next finger and stopped the bleeding.

Returning to Bernard he scarcely gave me a second glance. I have often wondered since what inspired Bernard to act this way, for all his training must have revolted against his kind action. Wolf came upstairs and ordered me down to the kitchen where the search was continuing. Willy, thickset in a leather full-length coat and wearing sort of plus four trousers was looking carefully at the ceiling light fixture. It was an ordinary, cheap bakelite pendant with a brown, twisted, cloth-covered flex leading to the bulb holder.

What had caught Willy's attention was the equally cheap bakelite two-way junction which led a wire down to the very ordinary plywood wardrobe with double doors standing at right angles to the wall as you entered the kitchen. He moved to the light switch and put it on, all the time looking up at the ceiling light fitting. When the bulb lit he opened the cupboard doors, both at the same time and glanced at all the coats and other garments on a lower shelf but did not disturb them.

What he thought the wire going to the cupboard did, I will never know, but he closed the doors and thoughtfully turned off the light too. Wireless sets in those days operated on valves which, took a few moments to warm up before the set began to operate, unlike the transistorised ones of today. Had Willy left the switch on for a few moments longer, he would have heard our Bush table model, wireless set, complete with 'magic eye' a clever, 1938 tuning gadget, come on air.

My mother did not lose her ability to act. She recalled that on the AGA at that moment was the contents of two tins of the iron rations taken from the bunker, this quite by coincidence. She indicated that the food would burn and one of the 'Gestapo' waved her up from the chair on which she was sitting to attend to it. She carried the pot to the sink and running the tap vigorously emptied a tasty meal of small dark beans, with pork in gravy down the drain unnoticed.

My father suddenly said, as if the 'Gestapo' did not matter, "Off you go to school or you will be late." How could I leave my mother and father at this time and I began to argue when Karl said, "Do as your father says, go to school". Looking back now I can see that my father was determined to spare me from what may follow. I kissed both my parents and left. When I got outside the kitchen into the entrance hall, I saw my bicycle and went to pick it up, but a rough hand gripped me and propelled me to the gate and threw me out. There was to be no cycle.

I can remember little or nothing about school that afternoon. I know I told my friends about the raid on our house, which they heard with awe, and the grapevine told me that all the boys who had taken the rifles had been caught. I hurried home, but with a sinking feeling opened the gate and went inside. Only my mother was in the kitchen, she told me that Dad had been taken away in a car by the 'Gestapo', but she did not know where he was. Francis was also in their hands. We hugged each other and could not believe how so very few short years ago, we had been a happy family enjoying motoring holidays together in various parts of England.

At last after a cup of carrot tea, she told me that she had to go out, but did not say where and she never did tell me. I found myself alone in the kitchen and the shock of it all came over me like a wave. I remember pulling one of the dark blue, corduroy covered easy chairs with its dark oak frame away from its position in front of the Aga and placing it against the side of the cooker as far back as it would go. I climbed on to it like a small injured animal and broke down completely.

We had always been a close family and my parents were sincere Catholics. I firmly believed in God and in prayer and how I prayed at that time. It was not the recitation of well-learnt prayers, but talking directly to God. I said that Hitler was an evil man who had done so much harm and that my father was so good. Why should Hitler and his men be allowed to succeed like this? I do not know how long I prayed, but it must have been for several minutes. Suddenly I felt my father's overcoat which was hanging on the wall beside my head and gripped it with heightened senses, breathing in the familiar smell I had often noticed when leaning against him as a younger boy as he drove us home late at night before this war. I pulled out a rosary and began to pray again, after a while I felt much better and got up and moved the chair back to its original position and sat down.

The knock at the door startled me. I got up, went through the kitchen door and opening the door leading into the entrance foyer I saw the partially obscured figure of a man through the reeded glass of the front door. My thoughts were in turmoil. Who could this be? I feared it was the return of the 'Gestapo'. Opening the door I saw a tallish man dressed in very clean, well -pressed civilian clothes of a black material. In his hand he held his hat and he wore an overcoat. " You must be Leo," he said, "Don't worry, I am a good friend of your father."

I thought from his appearance that he must have been a German officer off duty, but his manner and words made me realise that he was not. "May I come in?" he asked. I led him into the kitchen and told him that my mother was out and remember offering to make him a cup of carrot tea. He asked me gently how this was made, but refused it. Then sitting down in an adjoining chair he asked, "What is worrying you Leo?" I felt strangely warm and very much comforted and soon began to pour out all that had happened and that my deepest fear was that both my father and my brother would be shot. I knew by now that the 'Gestapo' had found radios my father was keeping for friends and that they had taken these and other items.

When I had finished, my 'father's friend' thought for a moment before he spoke and then said, "I want you to know that your father will be home in a few days and that he will be all right." I knew then that he must be a German Officer and guessed in a boyish way that he disliked the 'Gesatpo' as much as we did and knew something from official sources, but I never thought to question him about his name or indeed who he was. "What about Francis?" I asked. "Francis will be safe," he said, "but he will not be home for some time." Anxious about Francis, I pressed him to know when he would be home and I remember how hesitant he was before replying. "Not until the end of the war." These things I know were said to comfort me and then he got up and I saw him out. He would not wait to see my mother.

I could not wait for my mother to return to give her the good news. When she did come, perhaps half-an-hour later, I burst out with all my news. At last she understood clearly what I was saying and asked me who it was. Of course I did not know and tried to describe this gentleman, for that is what he was, while she attempted to fit the description to my father's known friends and acquaintances. None fitted in the slightest.

Several days passed. My bicycle had been taken by the Gestapo, as had all the other cycles. I do not know whether the Germans ever found out that all except mine were made up of parts of cycles we had 'liberated' from them. We had a store in a lockup garage in a back street in St. Helier. Hidden among the furniture were a few cycle parts. I had to have a cycle and so I took a small trolley to the store and came away with a selection of parts enough to assemble a cycle of sorts. As I went down Green Street on my way home, heavy of heart, one of the few cars on the road, a camouflaged Morris Ten of 1939 suddenly overtook me and slowed up alongside my trolley and me. I was shocked to see that it was Karl and one of his henchmen. He slowed right up and with lowered window looked right into my little pile without saying a word. I was stunned and felt weak. Just as suddenly as they had arrived, Karl waved at the driver and they drove off in the direction of the hotel. I feared what would happen when I arrived. I opened the gate with trepidation. They were not there.

All the prisoners were held in the German wing of the prison in Gloucester Street. I went there with my mother with a pitiful, small package of sandwiches for my father in the hope of seeing him. We were let into the prison precinct, but stopped by the guard at the gate and forbidden to enter. My mother asked him to give my father the food. He put down his rifle against the wall of his hut and took the package and roughly tore it open and then dismantled the sandwich. Spilling the contents to reveal a little pencil of the sort that used to be slipped down the spine of a pocket diary and a piece of paper.

My mother had hidden these without telling me so that I was very surprised. The guard yelled abuse in German at her and threw the sandwich on the ground. I felt very angry that he should treat my mother like this, then he let us go, but not before we had heard a disturbance above us in a sort of open corridor with barred gates and my father briefly became visible as he was wrestled away by the guards. He shouted above the din and commotion, "I'm all right Annie, I'm alright Annie, go home." We were pushed outside, confused and miserable. There was to be no visiting for either my brother or my father.

I began to sleep in my mother's room for comfort and security. Life felt insecure and very odd. We thought about my visitor and his message and wondered. Then one night a few days after the 'Gestapo' raid, I woke in the middle of the night to hear someone clambering up onto the balcony which skirted the bedroom. German soldiers had climbed up earlier on in the war to rip up wood, but my father had driven them off with an English Bobby's police whistle. I think they fled, because their own Military Police, the Feldgendarmerie, used a similar whistle and were a ruthless bunch. So I wondered whether the soldiers were back for firewood.

All of a sudden there was a figure silhouetted in front of the window and my father's voice saying, "Its all right Annie, let me in." We could not believe it. I hugged him and can still feel the cold touch of his cheek on mine, chilled by the night air. I had never felt so elated. He told us he had been asleep in his cell when the door had been opened and he had been taken downstairs to the guardroom, not knowing what was to happen to him. There had stood two of the 'Gestapo' who had signalled to him to follow them and had put him into their car. They had driven straight to the hotel with hardly a word and let him out at the gate and driven off. He could not get in through the gate and so had had to climb up onto the balcony. We told him that Francis had come home on his way to retrieve his rifle from where he had hidden it and he became very sad saying that he should not have done that, for now the 'Gestapo' had got real evidence against Francis.

Although we discussed my visitor, we never found out who he was or ever saw him again. However, the second part of his prediction was also true and Francis was safe, but did not come out of prison until Liberation Day, 9th May 1945.

'Karl'

The Fall of Berlin

Chapter Twenty   PLEASE TAKE DOWN THE FLAG

He was a very tall man, I remember, of course I was only a boy of fourteen, undernourished and not very tall for my age. Beside him my father seemed smaller too and there were other differences. After four years of German occupation, cut off from his Bank in Edinburgh, my father's clothes were threadbare and hung on his frame with ill fitting looseness. Our tall visitor was an officer from the tips of his riding boots to the peak of his cap. What I particularly remember about his uniform was the elegant cloak, which he wore, of plain, fine material fastened at his throat by Lionheaded clasps in bronze. I imagine he was a Colonel but he may have been a Major.

"Are you the owner of this house?" he asked in perfect English and in a polite tone of voice. "I am" my father replied. "Then may I ask you, Sir, as one gentleman to another, to take down the Flag. The ordinary soldier does not know how near the war is to ending and has not heard of the fall of Berlin. Already they are asking why the British flag should be flying and to save bloodshed I have come to ask you personally to take it down" and after a moments pause he smiled, inclined his head bowed slightly and added, "please".

I saw that my father had warmed to him. In a way I suppose he was pleased to have such a satisfactory ending to this escapade. The Union Jack had come into his possession right back at the start of the occupation in 1940. We were living, that is the family, my father and mother, my brother Francis and I, at the Marina Hotel on the seafront at Havre-des-Pas. My father had bought the Hotel in 1936 and had converted it from an Aquarium into the present day Hotel. Not far away in Green Street stood the redbrick British Army Barracks, typical of their kind.

Two storey, rectangular buildings with iron verandas across the front elevation. On their arrival in 1940, the German army had immediately commandeered hotels and other suitable buildings to billet their troops and the army barracks had been an obvious choice. There was an area of allotments immediately behind the barracks, the two buildings of which faced the road and the path to the allotments passed between them. We had obtained the use of one of the allotments, as we had no garden in which to grow food.

It must have been on a visit to this allotment that my father had seen a group of young soldiers kicking and trampling on the Union Jack, which they must have found somewhere in the building. As he came back he saw the flag lying on the ground and acting quickly on impulse, picked it up and undoing his overcoat, wrapped it around himself and closed his coat. No one stopped him and he walked back to the hotel. He vowed to himself that he would fly that flag again when Berlin fell. I imagine that he thought that when Berlin fell it would be the end of the war, but as it turned out, when Berlin fell we were still occupied by the German army with thousands of their troops in the island. Highly principled, when he heard the news on his radio he had taken out the flag from its hiding place, climbed to the third floor balcony, erected the short flagpole which had lain disused for four years of war and flew his Union Jack.

"Please" and the demeanour of the man touched my father. After all, this officer had come down from the Feldkommandturiat at College House on Mont Millais from which the flag must have been all too obvious. He had not threatened or used force. Perhaps in France or Belgium under these circumstances a squad of soldiers would have been despatched to shoot the foolish patriot. "Certainly," my father replied with that smile, which totally covered his face, wrinkling his eyes and making them twinkle. Our officer, for in the space of only a few moments we had formed an attachment to this honourable man who knew how to behave when facing defeat. With an elegant gesture, threw back his cloak from his right arm and shook my father's hand and, moving back a pace, saluted him. "Perhaps this war will end very soon and then we can all go back to our families," he said.

Then turning round he made his way from the hotel entrance the few paces to the high fence which shielded us from the road and passing through the gate he climbed into his car and was gone. My father smiled at my mother and at me, who had closely observed all that had gone on. We laughed with relief and pent up emotion, then he went upstairs and soon the flag was downstairs being handled by us all. We wondered how soon my brother would be released from prison where he had spent the last six months in solitary confinement at the age of sixteen.

Liberation -
What a difference the homely British Tommy!

Chapter Twenty-one   LIBERATION

With Francis in prison and my father released, but due to serve his sentence in May 1945, life became more circumspect. We did not know what the 'Gestapo' would get up to next. Francis was kept in solitary confinement for six months, until the older political prisoners kicked up a rumpus that a boy of seventeen should be held like this. It had an effect and Francis was transferred to the cells with the others. He soon made friends there and began to seem a good deal more cheerful when I saw him by courtesy of dear Sister Morgan.

Quite often Francis and I met alone in the casualty ward, as it was not always possible for my father and mother to make the journey. At these times he would question me anxiously about life at home and I would try to allay his concerns which were exaggerated by his confinement and separation. We rarely discussed the end of the war as we were all a little bemused by the fact that the Allied advance into Europe had not brought about the surrender of the Germans in the Channel Islands. However, Francis was kept primed with all the news we gleaned from the BBC

While in Gloucester Street, as we called the prison, my father had shared a cell with a young French Colonial officer, a Lieutenant from Algeria. He was in prison for refusing to work for the Germans. My father spoke about him quite often and although he never managed to get in touch with him after he came out of prison, my father was to meet up with him again on Liberation Day.

An attack from the sea had been mounted on the western flank of the invasion fleet in the early hours of D-Day. German E boats and minesweepers had been sent in from Brest, but this attack had been expected and the German 'fleet' was severely mauled and the remnants headed for safety. Three of the minesweepers gained cover in St. Helier harbour and might well have stayed there for the duration of the war, but their commander was a rabid nazi, determined to carry the war to the Allies. His marines were almost his personal guard and, it would seem, opposed to any softening of the Wermacht towards surrender.

With the Normandy peninsula fully liberated by the Allied forces, the German marines began to prepare their ships for a commando-style raid on the nearby coast. Superstructures were lowered and other alterations were made and the unit set off at night for Granville, some twenty miles away. Surprise was complete and the Americans, who held the region, were taken as they held a dance at the Granville Casino, totally unaware that the German commandos were on their way. You can imagine the scene as the Germans burst in with blackened faces and brandishing machine pistols. It was decided to take only senior American officers prisoner, as the german force did not have the capacity or the need to take all the servicemen who fell into their hands. Having sabotaged American materials they made the mistake of liberating German prisoners of war, from a nearby camp.

The Americans had a name for their generosity in the liberated areas and these Germans had been the beneficiaries of some of the American kindness. After all, many of the G.I.s were of German origin and could speak the language. With their usual casual approach to life and discipline, the Americans had won the respect of the P.O.W.s who were glad to be out of the war, which they could see was lost anyway.

Liberating these men and bringing them back to the privations of life for the Wermacht in occupied Jersey was like placing a time bomb in their ranks. Eventually they were having to punish these men for spreading unrest among the others.

However, the Germans, especially the marine units were jubilant at their easy success, but wisely decided not to repeat it. Rumours circulated that the marines wanted to take over the command of the islands and to adopt a more belligerent attitude towards the Allies. In fact, towards the end of the occupation, we believed that this was indeed the case and the arrival of H.M.S. Bulldog off Guernsey to accept the surrender of the garrisons was met with some arrogant Nazi displays of ill-humour. Meanwhile, a certain young, Algerian officer, now imprisoned in the old British administrative buildings on Pier Road, overlooking the harbour watched the return of the commando unit to St. Helier with great interest. He had seen the preparations being made and noted the absence of the vessels and now he saw them return. He wanted very much to go aboard them just to see what they had been up to.

With the issue of rations now virtually at an end, through lack of supplies, even the bread ration having finished, we were in a sorry plight. At last we learned of the Red Cross efforts to help us and of the arrival of the 'Vega' in Guernsey. We could not imagine what a Red Cross parcel would look like. My idea was something soft and rounded, wrapped in well creased, brown paper. What a surprise we were to get. My father and I took a little sack trolley to collect our parcels, for they were heavy and found clean, stiff cardboard boxes, well marked with Red Cross inscriptions. The load may have been heavy, but we made light of getting it home.

The first parcel was opened to reveal a wonderful sight of, not just food, but colourful labels and interesting packets and tins. The Canadian parcels were packed with typical transatlantic generosity. Nothing was second best, it was as though those responsible had gone into their biggest supermarkets and chosen all the best things to meet our needs. I must not let you think that the New Zealand parcels, which we also received, but later on, were inferior in any way, for they were not, but, reflecting the traditions of that country the goods were homely and full of nourishment, if packed in plainer tins. You would find Lamb stew and solid plain chocolate in a tin in the New Zealand box and 'off the shelf' chocolate and Spam in the Canadian. My father wanted to put the parcels away and struggle on as we were in case things got really bad, as if they were not bad enough already. There was such a howl of protest from Francis and me, the first parcels having arrived before Francis' imprisonment, that my father relented and we enjoyed the contents of our first, unforgettable parcel.

The Germans were not entitled to parcels, but walking along the beach behind 'Bagnoles' and 'Silvertide' we saw the unmistakable Red Cross tins lying in a pile on the sand underneath a window. How they achieved this I do not know, but I know what I saw then and how it angered us to think of it. Later on, when Francis was in prison, the men used to open their parcels while the German guards looked on and let them see the luxurious contents, especially the cigarettes. Otto and other guards had been fair to the prisoners, so the odd cigarette was handed to them.

As the news became better and better, we were elated, despite the straits we were in. We began to know with certainty that we would win the war. There was, however a niggling uncertainty about the Germans and especially about the Nazi marine unit. It was more than likely that they would refuse to surrender and put up a fight. How we detested them and you must remember that my brother and his friends in 'Gloucester Street' were at their mercy.

At about this time some of Francis friends who were imprisoned with him, made a daring escape over the prison wall and Donald Bell got away as did Frank Keiller who had been arrested demonstrating at the deportation of the British residents and had knocked out a German officer. 'Dicky' Williams was a well-built, athletic boy, a brilliant water polo player and he was in on the escape. Unfortunately, in jumping off the prison wall to the pavement below, he fractured both ankles and was taken by the guards and dragged back into the prison. Donald and Frank remained at large until the war ended.

The day neared when my father would have to return to prison to serve his sentence, but this now seemed unlikely. Then it seemed to come upon us in a rush, the German High Command had signed the articles of Unconditional surrender on Luneberg Heath and the war was nearly over. The death of Hitler, the fall of Berlin had all been unmistakable pointers along the way, but the actual surrender was something else and we wondered how the surrender of the Channel Islands would be effected. We were not forgetting our Nazi jailers.

May 8th, 1945 was a day I shall never forget. All parties and Christmases and every other happy event pale into insignificance before that lovely day. How can I hope to convey to you the feeling, the elation, it seemed the very scent of that day? To awaken that morning and to look out of your window and see not a German in view and to know that exciting things were going to happen, one after the other. One of the first things my father did was to place a large loudspeaker on the wall bordering the road and to plug it into a radiogram he had 'preserved'. Passers-by stopped to listen, all the news was good and when it was announced that Winston Churchill would address the nation, quite a large crowd gathered at the appointed time, for most people no longer had a radio set of their own. Quite a cheer went up when Churchill came to the famous, "our dear Channel Islands will soon be free." At last we knew.

I thought that my parents would want to leave the island at once, but to my surprise this was not the case. In fact we did not leave until 1946. However, my Uncle Bob, my father's older brother had other ideas and one of the first phone calls into Jersey came through the 'pub' across the road from the hotel. The landlord came hurrying over to ask my father to come and take a call from a Mr. Harris of Edinburgh. Uncle Bob was a man of few words, but choked with emotion, he told my father to get the next boat out to England and that he would meet us in Southampton or wherever with a large caravan and take us back to Scotland.

He must have been dreadfully worried about us throughout the war and this worry would have increased with the discovery towards the end of the war, of Nazi wrongdoing and atrocities throughout Europe. He could not understand my father's gentle refusal and calming words and thought he was mad. But we felt secure among the Jersey people who had proved so friendly and helpful over the last four years.

Through some bureaucracy, Francis was not to be released from Gloucester Street until May 9th although the war was over. This irked us considerably, but short of storming the prison there was not much we could do about it. We would have to be patient and look forward to tomorrow.

Wherever we went, the Germans had left in a hurry, ammunition, weapons and equipment lay around in bunkers and in their billets. Only their personal belongings had gone. Everyone we met was in high spirits, smiling and laughing and so willing to talk, not about the past, but about today and what was going to happen. The only sad ones were those who fraternised with the Germans and who skulked around their houses afraid to show their faces. Girls who had gone out with the Germans, those who had worked for them, and those who had gone out of their way to be their friends.

My father played his trump card when he took me down to Farsley, a little lane opposite the Marina Hotel, I think our end was called Havre-des-Pas Gardens. He slid back the doors of a lock up garage and there was a little, black B.S.A., 10 h.p. car shining brightly and ready to go. We climbed in and sat on the soft, green, leather and soon we were back at the hotel to collect my mother and to take her for a little spin. What joy to do it so openly, so freely? How it compared with our night ride to Trinity on Christmas Eve 1943. After this my father collected his Smith and Wesson revolver and tucked it into his belt beneath his jacket out of sight and with me sitting beside him, he drove to 'Silvertide' the headquarters of the 'Gestapo' to recover his stolen goods.

The 'Gestapo' were at home, but what a change in them, gone were the smart suits and waistcoats, these had been replaced with army uniforms. Now they were humble private soldiers and corporals. I waited in the car while my father went in, I was very nervous as I thought he meant to shoot them for what they had done to Francis and others, but no, he soon came out with Bernard of all people, now wearing a corporal's stripe. Bernard was very quiet and sat in the back of the car while we set off under his directions for Upper King's Cliff where the 'Gestapo' had a house and store. I was fiddling with a little, six inch long Union Jack on a steel pin and trying to fasten it to the inside of the windscreen, when my father told me to put it away. "Bernard has had enough already and there is no need to rub it in." he said.

On arrival at the 'Gestapo' house, we were met by more 'Gestapo' now dressed as soldiers and Bernard ordered them to restore our radios to us. Some of these were being kept by my father for friends and he was determined to return them. We went into a large conservatory and saw carefully documented pieces of evidence, all labelled in German, to tie them in with some offence. Our radios were quickly found and while the Germans happily carried them to the car and secured them to the luggage carrier, we glanced around. Two neat Browning automatic pistols lay close to hand and my father slipped one into his pocket, it was a lot more manageable than his concealed Smith and Wesson which made him look rather portly, despite the years of starvation. We soon left with Bernard who was dropped off at 'Silvertide', while we continued back to the hotel. There the car was unloaded.

Later on we drove into town and came back up Pier Road where, unknown to us a certain Algerian Lieutenant was standing with his compatriots behind barbed wire and still guarded by a solitary German, but without a gun. We passed the guard and noticed the small group of prisoners behind the barbed wire and my father noticed his young friend. We stopped and reversed. The German attempted to remonstrate as my father approached the group of men, but he would have none of it and ignored the guard. There was a very joyful reunion through a gap in the wire. The Lieutenant told him that they were being retained under guard as there were fears that his men would run amok, but as comrades of the Allies he and his men should be free. My father agreed with him and told him he would be back soon.

We drove back in the car to the Marina Hotel where my father picked up a large sledgehammer, which I still have. This was stood on the floor in the back of the B.S.A. and we set off back to Pier Road. This time the German guard made one futile effort to protest, but my father's German had improved during the war to the level of being able to make this poor soldier realise that he was not wanted. He made off at good speed for he could see that his charges were about to be freed and I think that he was nervous about his own position with them.

With a few blows on the chain which secured this rather flimsy wooden gate the way was open and out came about ten or twelve French Colonial soldiers. Instead of fierce gestures, they jumped about and laughed around my father who beamed happily at them. Then, one after the other they produced packets of cigarettes and I thought they were going to light up and smoke, but no, they began literally to pour the cigarettes like water over my father's head so that they trickled to the ground and fell in piles at his feet. After some minutes of utter happiness, the Lieutenant called them to order and they listened to him in their native language and then saluted and wandered towards St. Helier in ones and twos with no more discipline than football fans who have just enjoyed a home win.

The young officer clambered into the front of the car and asked to be taken to the Ommaroo Hotel where he made some report and then rejoined us. His first request was to go to the harbour and to go aboard the Granville raid ships. The harbour was a scene of disorder. Equipment lay abandoned everywhere. We walked through some temporary German huts erected on the New North Quay to find them strewn with handgrenades tipped out of their boxes. At last we came to the lead ship which was of several hundred tons, but had no crew or watch aboard it. The moorings were loose and a wooden ladder led from the quay at a steep angle to her deck. We were soon aboard, that is the Lieutenant and me, for my father did not fancy the climb down.

What excitement for the officer, this was a moment he had been waiting for and he enjoyed it. In the main cabin, probably the wardroom, rather small and barely furnished, a Schmeisser nine-millimetre machine pistol lay on the table. He picked it up and examined it to see that it was empty of ammunition. I found myself carrying the weapon. Then he hurried off to find a screwdriver and took the ship's clock complete with German Eagle. In a passageway we found the wireless room with a medium size, transportable radio transmitter set up to operate. This we packed up and carried to the ladder for it was of a good weight, perhaps twenty pounds or thereabouts.

Before leaving, we went onto the bridge and the ship's compass attracted his attention. This joined the transmitter at the foot of the ladder. By this time the ship was rising on the incoming tide and the unattended mooring ropes were allowing her to drift away from the harbour wall. As I climbed up to follow our friend, pushing the transmitter ahead of me, the ladder began to slip down the wall with my weight on it and by the time that I reached the top it was five feet below the land tie.

I knew that I was going to fall into the water together with the transmitter, but I need not have worried. A strong brown hand grabbed first the heavy radio and then me and I found myself safe and dry and looking into the laughing face of a happy Algerian. I believe he intended to take his souvenirs home with him, but after we had sat down together at the Marina and he recalled that it was time to go, he suddenly gave me all his treasures and left. He wrote to my father several months later and enclosed a photograph of himself and his father posing amid palm trees outside the family Hotel.

We sat up late that night, too excited to sleep. The feeling of utter happiness which had carried us along all day, would not desert us now. Sleep at last claimed us and we went to bed with the certainty that the Nazis would not be able to delay our Liberation in the next day or so and Francis would be home tomorrow.

May 9th, 1945 was a long continuation of the same happiness, white bread and no need to hoard our Red Cross parcel stock of food. The wireless now in full view talking at a volume to which we were not accustomed filled our thoughts with news of celebrations throughout Europe and North America. Early in the morning my father set off for the prison in the car and my mother and I stayed at home to make preparations to receive Francis. I am sure my father expected trouble at the prison as he took his revolver with him and was determined that Francis was coming out today. On arriving at the main gate, he was told by a subdued Otto that it was not yet time for release of the prisoners.

He was more than a little surprised to find himself looking down the barrel of rather a large calibre revolver and to be told to fetch Francis at once. Before he could move, however, one of the other guards, on seeing what was happening, ran up the flight of stairs and shouted out that Francis was to be released at once. Francis came down almost immediately, but they did not spend too much time in joyful reunion, as my father was still concerned about the attitude of the Germans, who he felt, could not be trusted. What a welcome there was when Francis reached the hotel. It did not seem possible that we had survived the war intact as a family despite deportation attempts, imprisonment and 'Gestapo.' We could only thank God for preserving us.

Driving through the countryside in the North of the island on our way to see the Richardson's, we were suddenly stopped by a German who waved from the doorway of a cottage. We stopped and he came hurrying over. "Moment, please, moment, please," he said and hurried back inside the cottage. Back he came with some tools and a tyre pump for a German vehicle. "Please, you take," he said, "War is over, war finished, is gut." He smiled happily and patted my father's shoulder through the open window of the car, before returning to his billet.

The crowds wandering aimlessly round the streets of St. Helier were blissfully happy and nowhere were they happier or more numerous than outside the Pomme d'Or Hotel. Just to the east of the Hotel near the Southampton we stayed to chat with a small group of soldiers from the Hampshire Regiment who were bivouacking in and around their vehicles. Their uniform was in strange contrast to that of the Germans, no leather, no eagles, just plain, simple cloth and webbing and good equipment.

Their voices too, lacked the guttural tones of the departing troops and soft Hampshire accents responded to the eager questions of the happy Jersey people. It was like heaven and so sudden that it was difficult to take in. The patient soldiers listened to tales of deprivation and often handed out their own cigarettes and sweets. Wonderfully there was not a German in sight and so began the long period of forgetting Karl and Wolf and hunger and fear, of forgetting the long walk up to Gloucester Street and curfews and blackouts. Peace had come at last to Jersey.

In the ensuing days, we saw the Germans, now a bedraggled crew, assembled at West Park for powdering with D.D.T. by means of a blower nozzle pushed up their sleeves and around their waists. The landing craft as we watched were out of sight around Noirmont Point and DUKW.s were ferrying the prisoners out to them. Large landing craft came in with the tide and dried out on the beach in St. Aubin's Bay. We walked around them and chatted to their crews marvelling at the technology. It was difficult to realise that they were ours and not the enemies'.

Newsreels were brought in to the Island so that we could see pictures of the War and its various incidents. The newspapers were difficult to take in for they were full of advertisements from manufacturers telling us that they would soon be back into peacetime production and stressing their wartime role. Surrounding these advertisements was more trivial news of the tabloids. Gradually we became acclimatised to it all, to the good food, the freedom of information, and the ability to move freely about and of course to speak our minds. Soldiers became less of a rarity and we came into close contact with them from time to time.

The need for transport saw my father's cars rapidly sell to willing buyers, among them State's Departments. Strangely enough, he took over the very store from which Francis had misappropriated the bag of German flour, the old 'Blue Coach' garage, from which to sell his cars. One amusing weekly event was the car auction held by Harold Deslandes in Oxford Road opposite the Masonic Temple. Many unlikely old veterans, such as the farmer's old friend, the Essex Super Six, went under his hammer to the cry of, "Been on the road since V.E. Day."

I remember seeing a chromeplated and blue Rudge Whitworth motorcycle appear each week to be knocked down to a new owner. I asked a knowledgeable friend if he knew why it came back so often. " When you buy it," he told me, "It seems to have good compression, but will not start. So you check the ignition and carburettor and still it will not start. Then you take off the cylinder head and there you find no piston, but a big bed spring, hence the good compression. You can't buy a piston for it, so you put it back into the auction in the hope of getting your money back."

There was much more happening in a similar vein as peace settled upon us gradually. The Channel Islands were declared an Export area and any new goods we wanted came off the export quota, which had to be operated by all British firms. So while Britain struggled under post-war austerity, Jersey basked in the liberal supply of many luxury items. It was in this atmosphere that the Marina Hotel was sold and we returned to our family in Edinburgh to find our house in Morningside just as we left it in 1939. To go down into our cellar and to see all our boys' books, Meccano sets and other toys, was like seeing yourself in a mirror, knowing it was a reflection of your former self before the German experience.

Francis and I soon found ourselves back at school, boarding at the Salesian College in Cowley, Oxford. Lying in the dormitory at night, listening to the shunting of trains carried on the still night air; our minds would often wander back to other times. Could all this have really happened?

A shower of cigarettes -
The French Colonial
Troops are released.

My Father and Mother and Francis with our 'Replacement' Rover in 1946.

Home at last six years later - our house in Edinburgh 1946.

About the Author

Andrew Leo Curtis Harris was born in Edinburgh in 1930. His parents, John Francis Winn-Harris and his wife Anne, were in business running a successful garage in Blackhall on the outskirts of the city. He is the younger of two boys, his brother John Francis having been born in 1927. Both boys went to the Benedictine Preparatory School in Canaan Lane in Morningside and were to go to the boarding school at Fort Augustus in the Highlands. The war and the occupation of the Channel Islands in 1940 by the Germans intervened. Five years later after suffering much deprivation and the imprisonment of his father and brother, Leo found himself with Francis at the Salesian College, Cowley, Oxford. Later he went on to qualify as a teacher after some time as a student at St. Mary's, Twickenham and later at Goldsmith's'.

He married Yvonne Chevalier in 1963 and has two daughters, Alison & Frances. He taught from 1952 at St Helier Boy's School and Les Quennevais School, where he was head of Art from 1965 until his retirement in 1989. He then taught at both Victoria College and Jersey College for Girls until 1998.

Now retired, he lives with Yvonne in St Peter's and enjoys sailing, writing, his cars and not least his family and five grandchildren, Ben, Meredith, Harry, Laurence and Curtis.